EVALUATION
OF CRIMINAL
RESPONSIBILITY

BEST PRACTICES IN FORENSIC MENTAL HEALTH ASSESSMENT

Series Editors

Thomas Grisso, Alan M. Goldstein, and Kirk Heilbrun

Series Advisory Board

Paul Appelbaum, Richard Bonnie, and John Monahan

Titles in the Series

Foundations of Forensic Mental Health Assessment, *Kirk Heilbrun, Thomas Grisso, and Alan M. Goldstein*

Criminal Titles

Evaluation of Competence to Stand Trial, *Patricia A. Zapf and Ronald Roesch*

Evaluation of Criminal Responsibility, *Ira K. Packer*

Evaluation of Capacity to Confess, *Alan M. Goldstein and Naomi Goldstein*

Evaluation of Sexually Violent Predators, *Philip H. Witt and Mary Alice Conroy*

Evaluation for Risk of Violence in Adults, *Kirk Heilbrun*

Jury Selection, *Margaret Bull Kovera and Brian L. Cutler*

Evaluation for Capital Sentencing, *Mark D. Cunningham*

Eyewitness Identification, *Brian L. Cutler and Margaret Bull Kovera*

Civil Titles

Evaluation of Capacity to Consent to Treatment, *Scott Y.H. Kim*

Evaluation for Guardianship, *Eric Y. Drogin and Curtis L. Barrett*

Evaluation for Personal Injury Claims, *Andrew W. Kane and Joel Dvoskin*

Evaluation for Civil Commitment, *Debra Pinals and Douglas Mossman*

Evaluation for Harassment and Discrimination Claims, *William Foote and Jane Goodman-Delahunty*

Evaluation of Workplace Disability, *Lisa D. Piechowski*

Juvenile and Family Titles

Evaluation for Child Custody, *Geri S.W. Fuhrmann*

Evaluation of Juveniles' Competence to Stand Trial, *Ivan Kruh and Thomas Grisso*

Evaluation for Risk of Violence in Juveniles, *Robert Hoge and D.A. Andrews*

Evaluation for Child Protection, *Karen S. Budd, Jennifer Clark, Mary Connell, and Kathryn Kuehnle*

Evaluation for Disposition and Transfer of Juvenile Offenders, *Randall T. Salekin*

EVALUATION OF CRIMINAL RESPONSIBILITY

IRA K. PACKER

OXFORD
UNIVERSITY PRESS

2009

OXFORD
UNIVERSITY PRESS

Oxford University Press, Inc., publishes works that further
Oxford University's objective of excellence
in research, scholarship, and education.

Oxford New York
Auckland   Cape Town   Dar es Salaam   Hong Kong   Karachi
Kuala Lumpur   Madrid   Melbourne   Mexico City   Nairobi
New Delhi   Shanghai   Taipei   Toronto

With offices in
Argentina   Austria   Brazil   Chile   Czech Republic   France Greece
Guatemala   Hungary   Italy   Japan   Poland   Portugal   Singapore
South Korea   Switzerland   Thailand   Turkey   Ukraine Vietnam

Copyright © 2009 by Oxford University Press, Inc.

Published by Oxford University Press, Inc.
198 Madison Avenue, New York, New York 10016
www.oup.com

Oxford is a registered trademark of Oxford University Press

Packer, Ira K.
Evaluation of criminal responsibility / Ira K. Packer.
p. ; cm. — (Best practices in forensic mental health assessment)
Includes bibliographical references and index.
ISBN 978-0-19-532485-3
1. Insanity (Law) 2. Criminal liability. I. Title. II. Series.
[DNLM: 1. Forensic Psychiatry. 2. Insanity Defense.
3. Interview, Psychological—methods. W 740 P119e 2009]
RA1151.P33 2009
614'.1—dc22

2008041067

9 8 7 6 5 4 3 2 1

Printed in the United States of America
on acid-free paper

About Best Practices in Forensic Mental Health Assessment

The recent growth of the fields of forensic psychology and forensic psychiatry has created a need for this book series describing best practices in forensic mental health assessment (FMHA). Currently, forensic evaluations are conducted by mental health professionals for a variety of criminal, civil, and juvenile legal questions. The research foundation supporting these assessments has become broader and deeper in recent decades. Consensus has become clearer on the recognition of essential requirements for ethical and professional conduct. In the larger context of the current emphasis on "empirically supported" assessment and intervention in psychiatry and psychology, the specialization of FMHA has advanced sufficiently to justify a series devoted to best practices. Although this series focuses mainly on evaluations conducted by psychologists and psychiatrists, the fundamentals and principles offered also apply to evaluations conducted by clinical social workers, psychiatric nurses, and other mental health professionals.

This series describes "best practice" as empirically supported (when the relevant research is available), legally relevant, and consistent with applicable ethical and professional standards. Authors of the books in this series identify the approaches that seem best, while incorporating what is practical and acknowledging that best practice represents a goal to which the forensic clinician should aspire, rather than a standard that can always be met. The American Academy of Forensic Psychology assisted the editors in enlisting the consultation of board-certified forensic psychologists specialized in each topic area. Board-certified forensic psychiatrists were also consultants on many of the volumes. Their comments on the manuscripts helped to ensure that the methods described in these volumes represent a generally accepted view of best practice.

The series' authors were selected for their specific expertise in a particular area. At the broadest level, however, certain general principles apply to all types of forensic evaluations. Rather than repeat those fundamental principles in every volume, the series offers them in the first volume, *Foundations of Forensic Mental Health Assessment*. Reading the first book, followed by a specific topical book will provide the reader both the general principles that the specific topic shares with all forensic evaluations and those that are particular to the specific assessment question.

The specific topics of the 19 books were selected by the series editors as the most important and oft-considered areas of forensic assessment conducted by mental health professionals and behavioral scientists. Each of the 19 topical books is organized according to a common template. The authors address the applicable legal context, forensic mental health concepts, and empirical foundations and limits in the "Foundation" part of the book. They then describe preparation for the evaluation, data collection, data interpretation, and report writing and testimony in the "Application" part of the book. This creates a fairly uniform approach to considering these areas across different topics. All authors in this series have attempted to be as concise as possible in addressing best practice in their area. In addition, topical volumes feature elements to make them user-friendly in actual practice. These elements include boxes that highlight especially important information, relevant case law, best-practice guidelines, and cautions against common pitfalls. A glossary of key terms is also provided in each volume.

We hope the series will be useful for different groups of individuals. Practicing forensic clinicians will find succinct, current information relevant to their practice. Those who are in training to specialize in forensic mental health assessment (whether in formal training or in the process of respecialization) should find helpful the combination of broadly applicable considerations presented in the first volume together with the more specific aspects of other volumes in the series. Those who teach and supervise trainees can offer these volumes as a guide for practices to which the trainee can aspire. Researchers and scholars interested in FMHA best practice may find researchable ideas, particularly on topics that have received insufficient research attention to date. Judges and attorneys with questions about FMHA best practice will find these books relevant and concise. Clinical and forensic administrators who run agencies, court clinics, and hospitals in which litigants are assessed may also use some of the books in this series to establish expectancies for evaluations performed by professionals in their agencies.

We also anticipate that the 19 specific books in this series will serve as reference works that help courts and attorneys evaluate the quality of forensic mental health professionals' evaluations. A word of caution is in order, however. These volumes focus on best practice, not what is minimally acceptable legally or ethically. Courts involved in malpractice litigation, or ethics committees or licensure boards considering complaints, should not expect that materials describing best practice easily or necessarily translate into the minimally acceptable professional conduct that is typically at issue in such proceedings.

The present volume describes one of the most important, complex, and controversial forensic evaluations in forensic psychiatry and psychology. The notion of "insanity"—that it is unfair to hold "mentally impaired" people fully and criminally responsible for transgressions—is very old. It arises in the earliest recorded legal records of many civilizations. European and American law have long relied on information from medical experts to identify those who might qualify for this exemption from responsibility. The early identity of forensic psychiatry was substantially shaped by its ability to address criminal responsibility, through the scholarly contributions of its founders (such as Isaac Ray's 1838 *Treatise on the Medical Jurisprudence of Insanity*), as well as their testimony in those famous 19th-century cases that established some of our current legal definitions of insanity. Forensic psychologists joined forensic psychiatrists as insanity examiners later in the 20th century.

Despite this long history, the concepts associated with criminal responsibility are still complex and difficult to define. Nevertheless, in recent years, the field has developed a greater consensus regarding essential data collection methods, as well as how to manage the type of reasoning that is required to fit data to the legal definitions. This volume offers guidance for the forensic mental health examiner, based on tradition as well as the latest developments for improving practice in criminal responsibility evaluations.

Thomas Grisso
Alan M. Goldstein
Kirk Heilbrun

Acknowledgments

The questions posed about how to respond to criminal behavior by individuals who may be mentally disordered are intriguing from legal, moral, and psychological perspectives. I have learned a great deal from writing this book, and I want to thank the editors of this series, Tom Grisso, Alan Goldstein, and Kirk Heilbrun for honoring me by inviting me to participate. They also contributed substantively to this book. First, the edits and feedback provided by Tom (primary editor for this book) and Alan (secondary editor) were extremely helpful. Second, as I was writing, I often imagined how Tom, Alan, and Kirk would respond to certain points, and this always forced me to articulate my ideas more clearly.

I especially want to thank Steve Bank, the external reviewer for this book. His detailed comments were extremely helpful in clarifying a number of important nuances, as well as forcing me to rethink some crucial points. I appreciate his sharing his expertise and his willingness to take the time to discuss the issues with me at length. My thanks also go to Julia TerMaat, the developmental editor from Oxford University Press, for her contributions to make this book more readable and user friendly.

I am appreciative of my many forensic psychology and psychiatry colleagues, both in Massachusetts and across the country, from whom I have learned a great deal. I value the opportunity to consult with such outstanding colleagues and discuss complicated practice and ethical issues. I particularly rely on the extremely sophisticated and thoughtful responses that come, almost daily, from my colleagues on the American Academy of Forensic Psychology's listserv. Discussions with my psychiatric colleague, Debra Pinals, of some of the "minutiae" of forensic work, such as what does the term "wrongfulness" mean, have come in very handy in writing this book. But, of course, I have learned even more from my students, the Forensic Psychology and Psychiatry Postdoctoral Fellows at the University of Massachusetts Medical School. Their inquisitiveness, thoughtful and challenging questions, and thirst for knowledge have forced me to ponder many of the issues discussed in this book.

There are also some people whose contributions are more global. Having spent almost 30 years as a forensic psychologist working primarily in the criminal arena, I have often had to deal with the tragic and cruel aspects of life. I have been able to maintain a balanced perspective on life and keep my own "sanity" due to in large part to my wonderful family. I am grateful to my wife Sharon, my sons Ben, Daniel, and Avi, and my daughter-in-law Aviva for serving as a daily reminder of the wonderful and beautiful aspects of human nature.

Last, but not least, this book is dedicated to the two people to whom I owe the most: my mother, Rosalind, and my father of blessed memory, Ben. In particular, I appreciate how hard they worked to ensure that I received a top-quality education. It is thanks to their willingness to sacrifice that I have been able to achieve whatever successes I have in life.

Ira Packer

Contents

FOUNDATION

The Legal Context | 1

The Purpose of the Insanity Defense

The issue of legal and moral blameworthiness for violations of established laws is complex and controversial. It would be much simpler if individuals were considered guilty of crimes simply based on the nature of the act (the term used in the American legal system, borrowed from the Latin, is *actus reus* or "bad act"). However, even a cursory exploration of this area reveals that such a model would violate commonsense criteria.

For example, if Mr. Jones, while driving his car, strikes and kills Mr. Smith, is he guilty of a crime? It depends. Did Mr. Jones deliberately aim his car at Mr. Smith? Had they been involved in an argument right before the incident? Had Mr. Jones ever threatened to harm Mr. Smith? If the two parties were strangers, was Mr. Jones intoxicated at the time and hit Mr. Smith because he was driving erratically and did not see him? Had Mr. Jones been speaking on his cellphone at the time and become distracted? Was Mr. Jones driving carefully and had to swerve to avoid an oncoming truck, thus inadvertently striking Mr. Smith?

In all these scenarios, Mr. Jones committed the same act; the differences between the scenarios revolve around his mental state and his intentions. The decision about whether or not Mr. Jones is guilty of a criminal act, and if so, the severity of the crime, will be contingent upon whether he is deemed to have had *mens rea*, or "guilty mind." If it is determined that Mr. Smith intended to kill Mr. Smith, he is likely to be convicted of murder. The degree of murder is likely to hinge on an assessment of whether it was pre-meditated or not. If he were intoxicated or negligent in his driving, he is likely to be convicted of manslaughter. And, if it were determined that this was an accident beyond his control, he will not be found guilty of any crime.

The situation becomes more complex when a claim is made that the individual's lack of *mens rea* was due to a mental impairment. Many additional questions arise in such cases. What is the threshold for severity of the mental disorder? How do we determine the functional impairments that will be considered relevant to absolving the individual from culpability? How do we know the disorder is genuine?

Historical Basis for the Insanity Defense

Most jurisdictions in the United States have provisions for acquittal of defendants who are deemed legally insane. All jurisdictions have provisions for consideration of the impact of mental status on elements of the alleged crime or on the degree of culpability. This is not a modern concept. The Hebrew *Mishna* (almost 2,000 years ago), for example, recognized that certain individuals, due to their mental impairments, would be excused from *criminal responsibility* (CR). Included in this category were young children and individuals who today would be called "mentally ill" or "mentally retarded." Various terms were subsequently used in Anglo-Saxon law, including references to "lunatics" and "idiots," terms that apparently were assumed to have a commonsense meaning (that is, not requiring specialized expertise to diagnose). Similarly, in 18th-century England, what has become known as the "wild beast" standard was proposed: "a man must be totally deprived of his understanding and memory, and doth not know what he is doing, no more than an infant, brute, or a wild beast" (*Rex v. Arnold*, 1724). This standard required absolute impairment ("totally deprived").

The next section of this chapter describes the evolution of standards for insanity across the past 200 years. Despite those efforts, the insanity defense remains a very controversial topic. This is due, in part, to misunderstandings about the concept, the

INFO

Despite public perception, the insanity defense is seldom employed. Furthermore, it is frequently unsuccessful when used.

prevalence of its use, and the consequences for those who are found insane. There is public confusion about how someone who actually committed an act can be found *Not Guilty by Reason of Insanity* (NGRI). Furthermore, the public overestimates how often the insanity defense is used and thinks that insanity acquittees avoid negative consequences (e.g., Pasewark & Pantle, 1979; Steadman et al., 1993). As Appelbaum (1982) noted: "the public's perception that mentally ill offenders are being processed through a revolving-door system that rapidly returns to the streets those acquitted on grounds of insanity has provoked calls for reform" (p. 14). This public outcry has affected public policy, despite the inaccuracy of the perception.

In contrast to these public fears, it is estimated (Melton et al., 2007, summarizing data from studies across a number of jurisdictions) that only one-tenth of 1% of all felony cases (i.e., 1 out of every 1,000 cases) involves an insanity plea and, of those, only about a quarter are successful. Thus, the insanity defense is rarely raised and, when raised, is not often successful. Nevertheless, public opinion, and legislative action, are influenced to a great degree by the infrequent, but highly publicized case (what is known as the "representativeness heuristic," Kahneman, Slovic, & Tversky, 1982). This contributes to the misperception that the insanity defense is overused and abused.

Realities of the Outcome of the Insanity Defense

Similarly, the public has a tendency to see the insanity defense as a way for the defendant to "get away with it." Yet, a defendant found NGRI may end up spending more time in the hospital than he would have spent incarcerated if convicted. Consider the case of Mr. Jones (*Jones v. U.S.*, 1983), who was found NGRI of larceny. In 1975, Mr. Jones was arrested for attempting to steal a jacket from a department store and was arraigned in the District of Columbia Superior Court on a charge of attempted petit larceny,

CASE LAW

Jones v. U.S. (1983)

- After being found NGRI, Jones was committed to a psychiatric hospital and remained committed for a period longer than the maximum sentence he would have received had he been convicted.

- Jones appealed, claiming that his due process rights were violated by his commitment extending beyond the maximum sentence.

- The U.S. Supreme Court rejected Jones's claim, declaring that no correlation exists between the length of criminal sentence one would have received if convicted and the length of confinement required for treatment and protection.

- The Court also ruled that insanity acquittees could be subjected to more stringent standards for release than individuals civilly committed.

a misdemeanor punishable by a maximum prison sentence of 1 year. Jones subsequently pled not guilty by reason of insanity. The prosecution did not contest the plea, and the judge found him NGRI and sent him to St. Elizabeth's Hospital for an evaluation. At a hearing 50 days later, the District of Columbia Superior Court found that the Mr. Jones was mentally ill and dangerous, and ordered his commitment to the hospital. Per the D.C. statute, the burden then shifted to Jones to prove by preponderance of the evidence (that is, more likely than not) that he was no longer mentally ill or dangerous. The maximum sentence he had faced for conviction was 1 year, but he was committed for significantly longer than that (his case was heard by the Supreme Court in 1983). He therefore appealed, arguing that it was unconstitutional for him to be deprived of liberty as an insanity acquittee for longer than the sentence he would have received if convicted.

The Supreme Court rejected his claim, ruling that no relationship existed between the maximum sentence an insanity acquitee would have faced and the length of his psychiatric hospitalization. Their rationale was that

> The length of a sentence for a particular criminal offense is based
> on a variety of considerations, including retribution, deterrence,

and rehabilitation. However, because an insanity acquittee was not convicted, he may not be punished. The purpose of his commitment is to treat his mental illness and protect him and society from his potential dangerousness. There simply is no necessary correlation between the length of the acquittee's hypothetical criminal sentence and the length of time necessary for his recovery. (p. 369)

Thus, the length of confinement of insanity acquittees may exceed the period of incarceration they would have been subject to if they had been found guilty. Furthermore, a number of states have instituted *conditional release* programs for insanity acquittees. This means that, even after release from a psychiatric hospital, these acquittees are subject to restrictions and conditions placed upon them in the community, including continuing mental health treatment, abstaining from substance abuse, and other terms similar to probationary conditions for convicted defendants.

Several jurisdictions with conditional release programs have followed up acquittees in the community (e.g., Wiederanders, Bromley, and Choate, 1997). Results from these studies indicate that insanity acquittees are less likely than those convicted to recidivate, particularly for violent crimes. An encouraging finding is that those conditionally released are more likely to be rehospitalized rather than reincarcerated. This suggests that the conditional release programs are effective in intervening early with mental health treatment, rather than allowing an individual to decompensate to the point that he picks up new criminal charges. The realities related to the insanity defense, therefore, are quite different from the often-mistaken public perception that it is overused and that it results in increased risk to the public.

Consequences of Abolishing the Insanity Defense: Data From Montana

It is instructive, in this context, to consider the consequences in Montana, which abolished the insanity defense in 1979. The sociologist, Henry Steadman, and his colleagues (Steadman et al., 1993) compared data from the periods pre (1976–1979) and post

(1980–1985) abolition. Although, by definition, there were no insanity acquittees after 1979, the number of defendants adjudicated as *Incompetent to Stand Trial* (IST) increased significantly after abolition. Their conclusion was that the system responded in this way to the phenomenon of severely mentally ill individuals who violated the law and who were not considered criminally blameworthy. Once the option of insanity acquittal was removed, the alternative of adjudication as incompetent was more widely used. The long-term disposition was the same; mentally ill individuals were psychiatrically committed rather than incarcerated in penal institutions. This reinforces the principle underlying the insanity defense: a class of individuals exists who are mentally impaired and thus cannot be held to the same level of accountability as the majority of citizens. One way or another, societies must accommodate to this reality and develop laws that provide for alternative dispositions.

These data are relevant because they highlight the important idea that the forensic evaluation is embedded within a legal and social context. This is useful for the forensic evaluator to keep in mind regarding the attitudes that jurors typically bring to the courtroom. The issue of CR is ultimately not a psychological concept; it is a legal and moral one.

The Evolution of Legal Standards for Insanity

Unlike the legal concept of *competence to stand trial* (referring to a defendant's current capacities to participate in a trial), definitions of insanity are concerned with the defendant's past mental state (i.e., at the time of the alleged offense). The legal system's efforts to develop and apply legal standards defining insanity have resulted in several different definitions, so that different jurisdictions employ somewhat different standards. Appendix A identifies the legal standards for insanity in each of the states, as well as in the federal system. We will return to this table at the end of this section, which describes the origins and legal precedents for the major standards currently employed in the United States.

The M'Naghten Standard

The modern underpinning for the insanity defense standards prevalent in most U.S. jurisdictions stems from the case of Daniel M'Naghten in England in 1843. (For a detailed discussion of the M'Naghten case, see Moran, 1981.) M'Naghten was acquitted by reason of insanity of killing the secretary of the leader of the Tory party, Sir Robert Peel (who was the target of the assassination). Public outrage at the verdict resulted in new criteria for the insanity defense being established in England (known as the *M'Naghten standard*). This standard includes the following criteria:

> To establish a defense on the ground of insanity, it must be proved that, at the time of the committing of the act, the party accused was laboring under such a defect of reason, from disease of the mind, as not to know the nature and quality of the act he was doing or if he did know it, that he did not know he was doing what was wrong. (M'Naghten case, 1843)

This has come to be known as the "right–wrong test" and was adopted in many jurisdictions in the United States. One of the criticisms of this standard (e.g., American Law Institute [ALI], 1985) has been its one-sided focus on the "cognitive" aspect (i.e., focused on "knowing" and ignoring the impact of various emotional states on actions). As a result of this focus, the standard fails to take account of possible impairments in volitional control. Some states responded to this latter criticism by incorporating what is known as the "irresistible impulse" test—that is, a defendant can also be found insane if she acted in response to an irresistible impulse. However, this was not a workable solution because of the difficulty in developing criteria for assessing this standard. Specifically, how could mental health professionals and

CASE LAW

M'Naghten case (1843)

● Established a standard that has been adopted in many U.S. jurisdictions

● Included as criteria for insanity whether the defendant

a. did not know the nature and quality of the act, or

b. did not know that what he was doing was wrong

the legal system distinguish between an impulse that *could* not be resisted versus an impulse that *was* not resisted?

The "Durham" Rule

It is instructive to consider the approach to defining legal insanity taken by the Federal Court of Appeals for the District of Columbia in 1954. In an opinion authored by Judge David Bazelon (*Durham v. U.S.*, 1954), the court adopted the *product standard*. This standard stated that a defendant would be found NGRI if the criminal behavior was deemed to be the "product of mental disease or mental defect" (p. 874–875). The rationale for the change was twofold: (a) concern that the M'Naghten standard was too narrow and (b) concern that mental health professionals (then almost always psychiatrists) were being forced to focus on the legal criteria, which negatively impacted their ability to provide the courts with their true expertise, clinical assessments, and analyses. *Durham*'s language was intended to give the forensic expert more leeway in providing the courts with relevant mental health testimony.

This change was well-intentioned, but in practice it did not result in clearer, more appropriate testimony. The standard did not provide adequate guidance regarding what constituted a mental disease or defect from a legal perspective, thus resulting in lack of consistency from the psychiatric community. The meaning of "mental disease" for those mental health professionals who were assessing patients in a clinical context to provide treatment was different from its meaning for purposes of legal determinations. Recognizing this, a U.S. Court of Appeals clarified the legal definition in the case of *McDonald v. United States* (1962), referring to "any abnormal condition of the mind which substantially affects mental or emotional processes and substantially impairs behavior controls" (p. 851). Notably, this definition incorporated a reference to impairment in behavioral control, thus stepping back somewhat from the more open-ended

CASE LAW

Durham v. U.S.
(1954)

- Put forth the "product standard," in which defendants would be found NGRI if their criminal behavior was a product of mental disease of defect

- Was not clear on what constituted a mental disease or defect from a legal perspective

approach encouraged in *Durham*. However, even this change did not suffice to solve the difficulties with this standard; it still did not provide guidance about how to determine whether a particular criminal behavior was indeed the "product" of the symptoms of a mental illness, as opposed to personality or contextual variables. Thus, even if it were established that a defendant was suffering from a mental illness at the time of the offense, this did not necessarily imply that the particular criminal behavior was the result of the mental illness. Furthermore, this definition still did not resolve internal disputes within psychiatry about what constituted a mental disease. So, in 1972, the same Circuit Court reversed itself, rescinded the *Durham* standard, and adopted the *American Law Institute (ALI) standard* for its jurisdiction (*U.S. v. Brawner*, 1972).

American Law Institute Standard

The ALI, in 1962, proposed a Model Penal Code (MPC) that included a standard for the insanity defense. The proposed language indicated that a defendant would be found NGRI if "as a result of mental illness or mental defect he lacked substantial capacity either to appreciate the wrongfulness of his conduct or to conform his conduct to the requirements of the law" (ALI, 1985).

APPRECIATION OF WRONGFULNESS

How was this new standard different from the two previous standards—M'Naghten and irresistible impulse? The two critical words in this part of the definition are "appreciate" and "wrongfulness." The concept of appreciation was meant to broaden the conceptualization beyond intellectual knowledge to incorporate the need for an awareness of the significance of the act. The commentary that accompanied the development of the standard noted that the M'Naghten standard "does not readily lend itself to application of emotional abnormalities"

INFO

Note that the ALI standard is disjunctive: a defendant will be considered insane if impairment exists in *either* ability to appreciate (which is often referred to as the "cognitive prong") *or* in ability to conform conduct (which is often referred to as the "volitional prong").

(ALI, 1985, p. 166). The use of the term "wrongfulness" connotes that the focus is on the defendant's appreciation of the moral wrongfulness of the behavior, not simply that it is legally prohibited, or criminal (e.g., Fingarette, 1972). How this latter term has been applied in a number of legal jurisdictions will be discussed in more detail in Chapter 2.

ABILITY TO CONFORM CONDUCT

Another significant change in the MPC language was a shift from the term "irresistible impulse" to impairment "in ability to conform conduct." Although this may seem, on first impression, more like a semantic than a substantive difference, this change does have significant implications both conceptually and practically. Rather than focusing on the strength of the impulse to act, this formulation calls for an analysis of the individual's ability to exercise control over the impulse. In simplistic terms, one can think of this, analogously, as the difference between an "id" psychology and an "ego" psychology. The term "irresistible impulse" conjures up images of an "id" that produces overwhelmingly powerful impulses. The term "conform conduct," by contrast, focuses on the individual's capacities and resources to exert self-control and inhibit impulses. This analogy is not offered here in a literal sense, but rather as a way of distinguishing the different terms.

In practice, there had been great variability across jurisdictions in how the "irresistible impulse" standard was understood, with some courts defining it more broadly to emphasize the lack of control and others in the narrower sense portrayed here (Goldstein, 1967). Nevertheless, as will be discussed in Chapter 2, the term "conform conduct" is more conducive to attempts to develop criteria relevant to impairment in volitional control. It is also noteworthy that, regarding both the cognitive and the volitional prongs of this definition, the defendant must lack "*substantial* capacity," a term that connotes a significant degree of impairment but not an absolute lack of ability.

EXCLUSION OF SOCIOPATHY

A caveat included in the ALI insanity standard states that the terms mental disease and mental defect "do not include an abnormality manifested only by repeated criminal or otherwise antisocial conduct." This language was specifically designed to prevent individuals who were then referred to as *sociopaths* (and who are now referred to as *psychopaths*) from using the insanity defense. It is important to appreciate that this exclusion represents a legal and moral determination, not *necessarily* a scientific one. Although many clinicians agreed with this distinction, which conceptualized sociopaths as able to appreciate that their behavior was wrong by societal standards but being undeterred by societal norms and the ensuing consequences, others argued that these individuals were so impaired in their ability to make moral decisions as to be considered mentally ill. Indeed, Cleckley's (1941) seminal work in this area was called *The Mask of Insanity*.

This issue came to prominence in the mid-1950s in what the D.C. Court of Appeals dismissively labeled the "weekend flip flop case" (*U.S. v. Brawner*, 1972, p. 978). A psychiatrist at St. Elizabeth's hospital in Washington, D.C. testified on a Friday that a patient did not have a mental disease, but rather was a "sociopath." On Monday, the psychiatrist reversed the testimony, indicating that in a meeting during the weekend it was determined "as an administrative matter" at the hospital that henceforth sociopathy would be considered a mental disease. The response to this lack of consistency in the clinical community led to the legal system settling the matter by fiat.

Hinckley Case and Its Aftermath

Similar to the M'Naghten case, the acquittal by reason of insanity of John Hinckley in 1983 of the attempted assassination of President Ronald Reagan (and the serious wounding of his press secretary, James Brady) led to calls for changes in the insanity defense in the United States (Steadman et al., 1993). One of the most pronounced changes was the retreat from the volitional

CASE LAW

Hinckley (1983)

- John Hinckley was acquitted by reason of insanity of the attempted assassination of President Ronald Reagan.

- Outcry over his acquittal led to a number of changes in the insanity defense, including a retreat in some jurisdictions from using the volitional prong.

prong ("conform conduct"), based on arguments that this was a more amorphous concept, less amenable to clear assessment. The general sense was that the jury was influenced in its decision primarily by the volitional prong (although no clear evidence supports that they would have convicted using only the cognitive prong). The American Psychiatric Association (1983) and the American Bar Association (1983) both endorsed this change. The American Psychiatric Association's position focused on the difficulties involved in determining whether a particular defendant could or could not refrain from acting, noting that "The line between an irresistible impulse and one not resisted is probably no sharper than that between twilight and dusk." The American Psychological Association (1984) argued that more research was needed before any changes could be recommended.

As of 2007, 16 states still incorporate the volitional prong in their definitions of insanity defense, whereas 29 states and the Federal system do not (four other states have abolished the defense, and New Hampshire continues to use the product standard). Appendix A contains a listing of the insanity defense standards in these jurisdictions. It is noteworthy that, although all jurisdictions that maintain an insanity defense (except New Hampshire) include a cognitive prong, variations appear in the terminology, for example in the use of terms such as "know" versus "appreciate." (However, as discussed by Steadman et al. [1993], the empirical data do not suggest that these differences in terminology affect the ultimate verdicts.) Other changes instituted following the Hinckley acquittal included shifting the burden of proof from the prosecution to the defendant, instituting an alternative verdict of *Guilty but Mentally Ill* (GBMI), and changing the dispositional alternatives for insanity acquittees (to make it easier to commit them for longer periods of time to confinement or community control).

BEWARE
Keep in mind that deciding whom to acquit of CR by reason of insanity is a moral and legal decision, not a clinical one.

The significance of the foregoing discussion is to demonstrate the relationship between the legal and mental health professions in developing standards for excusing defendants from responsibility for otherwise criminal behaviors. The basic concept that some individuals, due to mental impairments, will not be held criminally responsible is based on moral and legal considerations. In the modern era, the legal system has looked to mental health professionals to provide input regarding the nature of psychological processes and mental disorders that could bear on this issue. However, in the final analysis, the decision about which types of individuals to exclude from CR is a moral and legal one, not a clinical judgment. The forensic clinician's role is to provide the court with as thorough and accurate an assessment as possible of the defendant's mental status, focusing on those functional abilities relevant to the legal standard in the particular jurisdiction. Indeed, an individual with a specific diagnosis and clinical presentation may be considered sane if her offense were committed in one jurisdiction, but insane if it were committed in another jurisdiction, due to different legal definitions.

Guilty but Mentally Ill

In response to public concern about highly publicized cases (preceding the Hinckley verdict), the alternative verdict of GBMI was developed. The rationale for this new verdict was that it would allow jurors to recognize that a defendant suffered from a mental illness, without having to be persuaded to acquit by reason of insanity. The data on whether this verdict has indeed resulted in fewer insanity acquittals in the states in which is has been adopted is mixed (Steadman et. al, 1993).

Regardless of the utility of this verdict for producing the desired outcomes, it has been criticized for being deceptive and meaningless. For instance, research on this verdict in Michigan demonstrated that most GBMI verdicts were arrived at via plea bargain rather than through a jury trial (Smith & Hall, 1982). This suggested that defendants were being convinced to accept a plea bargain to be found mentally ill, when this did not translate into any practical advantage for them. Specifically, the word "but" in the verdict suggests some diminution of responsibility or punishment. However, none of the GBMI statutes include any provision for a lesser punishment, thus creating a misconception about the implications of this verdict (Petrella, Benedict, Bank, & Packer, 1985).

Interestingly, Utah uses the term Guilty *and* Mentally Ill, which is a more accurate terminology. Yet, in that jurisdiction, it does not result in a reduced sentence, but focuses on the defendant's mental state at the time of sentencing and need for treatment.

Forensic clinicians may be asked, in the context of a CR evaluation, to evaluate defendants in reference to the issue of GBMI— that is, simply to determine whether the person had a mental disorder at the time of the alleged offense, apart from an evaluation of its effect. In a sense, this issue is subsumed under an insanity evaluation, since the first element in all insanity statutes is whether the defendant was mentally ill at the time of the alleged offense. However, the evaluation may, in some jurisdictions, also involve an assessment of the defendant's mental state at the time of sentencing.

Diminished Capacity

In addition to the insanity defense, many jurisdictions provide for a *mens rea* defense, or a *diminished capacity defense*. This requires evidence of mental impairment related to the defendant's ability to form the required *intent* that is an element of the crime charged. Unlike the insanity defense, which is an affirmative defense (i.e., there is a presumption of sanity, unless the defendant specifically raises the issue of insanity), the prosecution has the burden of proving that the defendant had the requisite intent in order to convict. Furthermore, while insanity is a complete defense (i.e., if found insane, the defendant is not guilty), diminished capacity is typically a partial defense, leading to conviction on a lesser included offense. In addition, defendants acquitted by reason of insanity are subject to special conditions (such as involuntary psychiatric commitment), whereas no such provisions are associated with successful diminished capacity defenses.

The concept of diminished capacity relates to a distinction in the law between those crimes that are considered to require only "general intent" from those that require "specific intent." A diminished capacity defense relates only to crimes requiring a specific intent. Although these terms are not precisely defined, general intent has been associated with the concepts of negligence and recklessness, whereas specific intent has been linked to the

INFO

Diminished capacity is used only to defend against conviction of specific-intent crimes, which carry a higher penalty than general-intent crimes.

concepts of knowledge and purpose, as defined by the ALI's MPC (Melton et al., 2007). For example, first-degree murder, which requires deliberation, is considered a specific-intent crime, but the lesser included offenses of second-degree murder and manslaughter require only general intent (some states have limited the use of diminished capacity defenses to homicide cases). In addition, certain crimes specifically incorporate the term "intent" in the charges, thus making them specific-intent crimes (e.g., breaking and entering with intent to rape, as opposed to the general-intent crime of breaking and entering). A successful diminished capacity defense will typically result in the defendant being convicted of the general-intent crime, which carries a lower penalty.

DIMINISHED CAPACITY VERSUS DIMINISHED RESPONSIBILITY

The diminished capacity defense has been plagued by conceptual and practical problems. This defense has been notably referred to by Morse, in an influential paper (1979), as a "moral and legal conundrum." One of the core issues is in the use of the term "diminished capacity," which is easily confused with "diminished responsibility," implying impairments in the cognitive or volitional elements associated with the insanity defense, but at a lower level of severity (Clark, 1999; Morse, 1984; *U.S. v. Frisbee*, 1985; *U.S. v. Cameron*, 1990). Indeed, California, in a line of cases in the 1960s and 1970s (e.g., *People v. Conley*, 1966; *People v. Poddar*, 1974), explicitly expanded the concept to serve as a "mini-insanity defense." This development was influenced by the prominent forensic psychiatrist, Bernard Diamond. Diamond was reacting to the all-or-none nature of the insanity defense when dealing with mentally ill defendants. He believed that the diminished responsibility defense would allow a more nuanced approach to dealing with mentally ill individuals who are involved in the legal system, and "form the keystone of the bridge between psychiatry and law" (Quen, 1994, p. 81). This well-intentioned enterprise ultimately was unsuccessful, as the California legislature abolished this defense in 1981.

One of the contributors to this legislative decision was the case of Dan White, who successfully used the diminished capacity defense to obtain a conviction of voluntary manslaughter, rather than murder. Evidence indicated that he had entered the city hall in San Francisco with a loaded gun, took steps to avoid detection by security and metal detectors, and killed Mayor George Moscone, who had refused to reappoint him to a supervisory post. He then reloaded his gun and shot Harvey Milk, whom he blamed for advising the mayor not to reappoint him. One of the defense experts, in discussing White's state of mind, referred to his binging on junk foods, with resulting metabolic changes, as contributing to a depressive episode. This was picked up by the media, and the diminished capacity defense was ridiculed as the "Twinkie defense," although it is not clear whether this one element actually played a major role in the verdict. Nonetheless, California retreated from this expanded definition of diminished capacity and reverted to the narrower use of the term. Across other jurisdictions, a great deal of variability exists regarding this defense, including whether it is recognized at all, whether evidence of intoxication can be used to demonstrate lack of specific intent (which will be discussed in more detail in Chapter 2), and the role of mental health professionals in providing testimony on this issue, as discussed later in the case of *Clark v. Arizona* (2006).

INSANITY DEFENSE REFORM ACT

One of the ambiguities concerning the diminished capacity defense involved the Federal statutes, which were amended in 1984 in the wake of the Hinckley case. Congress enacted the *Insanity Defense Reform Act* (IDRA), which not only abolished the volitional prong of the insanity defense, but also included the statement that, other than the affirmative insanity defense, "mental disease or defect does not otherwise constitute a defense" (IDRA, §17). Although some lower courts initially interpreted this to mean that evidence of mental impairment or intoxication could not be presented to negate intent, several cases (e.g., *U.S. v. Frisbee*, 1985; *U.S. v. Pohlot*, 1987; *U.S. v. Cameron*, 1990) clarified the meaning of the statute. The courts ruled that the statute was intended only to bar affirmative defenses, in which the defendant would be excused for behavior due to mental illness (insanity defense), as opposed to situations in which the defendant was attempting to demonstrate that he did not commit one of the elements of the offense (diminished capacity). In the latter cases, evidence bearing on whether the defendant did or did not have the requisite intent was deemed relevant in federal jurisdictions. As will be discussed in Chapter 2, in some cases, the issue is not a question of *capacity*, but rather whether the defendant *did* form the intent.

Extreme Emotional Disturbance

Another partial defense used in a minority of jurisdictions (estimated at 11 by Kirschner, Litwack, & Galperin, 2004) is that of *extreme emotional disturbance* (EED). This defense stems from the ALI's MPC, and is considered a more expansive alternative to the existing defense of provocation. The latter defense provides for a murder charge to be reduced to manslaughter, if the defendant acted in the "heat of passion" in response to a provocation that would lead an ordinary person to lose control (e.g., an individual who discovers a spouse engaged in an act of infidelity, or someone who, in the context of a fight initiated by the victim, escalates and kills the other person). This is an objective standard—that is, whether the provocation that led to the homicide was one that would have inflamed the passions of a "reasonable" person. In contrast, EED allows for a subjective assessment of the provocation, from the defendant's perspective. The MPC language indicates that the homicide would be considered manslaughter rather than murder if it were "committed under the influence of extreme mental or emotional disturbance (EED) for which there is reasonable explanation or

INFO

Unlike the diminished capacity defense, the EED defense does *not* claim that the defendant was impaired in forming the intent of her actions, only that she did so under extreme emotional or mental disturbance.

excuse. The reasonableness of such explanation or excuse shall be determined from the viewpoint of a person in the actor's situation under the circumstances as he believes them to be" (ALI, 1985, Section 210.3[1][b]).

EED differs from the diminished capacity defense in that it does not involve impairment in capacity to form an intent. A defendant may fully intend the consequences of his actions, but can prevail with an EED defense if the trier of fact agrees that the defendant was experiencing a mental disorder or emotional instability that mitigated his responsibility. As such, this defense also differs significantly from an insanity defense, since less severe impairments would be considered relevant, and the defendant is still found guilty, but of a lesser offense. EED has been criticized as being overly broad because of the subjective component (e.g., Kahan & Nussbaum, 1996), although in a study of 24 defendants using the defense over a 10-year period in one county in New York, Kirschner and colleagues (2004), found that only nine were successful in avoiding a murder conviction. They concluded that defendants in that county were more likely to prevail if they could demonstrate that they acted out of an understandable fear that they (or someone close to them) were likely to be harmed by the victim.

Clark v. Arizona (2006)

As noted earlier, four states have abolished the insanity defense, and the Supreme Court has avoided addressing the issue of whether states are constitutionally required to allow such a defense. However, in the case of *Clark v. Arizona* (2006), the Supreme Court addressed a claim that Arizona's statute was unconstitutional because it eliminated one aspect of the M'Naghten standard. The case is worth reviewing in detail because it highlights the concept that although mental health expertise may inform legal policy concerning the insanity defense, it does not translate into any specific standard. This case is also instructive on a number of levels and will serve as a reference point for several issues related to the interface of mental health and the law regarding CR.

On June 21, 2000, Eric Clark was driving his truck in the early hours of the morning around a residential area, with loud music emanating from his truck. Officer Jeffrey Moritz responded to a complaint about Clark's behavior. The officer turned on his siren and emergency lights and Clark pulled over. The officer exited his marked patrol car and told Clark to stay where he was. Shortly thereafter, Clark shot the officer (who died of his wounds) and then ran away on foot. He was arrested later in the day, and the murder weapon was found stuffed into a cap. Clark was subsequently charged with first-degree murder based on the allegation that he had intentionally or knowingly killed a law enforcement officer.

At trial, Clark did not deny shooting the officer but claimed that he was not guilty by reason of insanity on the grounds that he suffered from paranoid schizophrenia. He provided both expert psychiatric testimony as well as lay witnesses to corroborate his symptoms of mental illness. For instance, in the year prior to the shooting, he exhibited bizarre behavior based on paranoid delusional beliefs. He believed that Flagstaff, Arizona was populated with aliens (including some who were impersonating government agents) who were trying to kill him. At his home, he had set up a fishing line with wind chimes and beads to alert him to intrusions by the aliens. A psychiatrist testified for the defense that Clark shot the officer in the context of his paranoid delusions, which prevented him from understanding that his acts were wrong.

The prosecution countered with lay testimony that Clark had told people a few weeks earlier that he intended to shoot police officers. Prosecutors presented evidence from a psychiatrist who agreed that Clark suffered from paranoid schizophrenia, but offered the opinion that Clark nevertheless was aware that his actions were wrong. The psychiatrist cited Clark's behavior of evading the police and hiding the gun, as well as his driving in circles with the music blaring (ostensibly to lure the police officer to the scene).

Clark was convicted of first-degree murder at a bench trial, with the judge concluding that, although he suffered from paranoid schizophrenia, this mental illness did not "distort his perception of reality so severely that he did not know his actions were wrong." Ultimately, his appeal was heard by the U.S. Supreme Court. Clark raised two main issues on appeal. The first was his claim that Arizona's definition of insanity was unconstitutionally narrow because it eliminated the first part of the M'Naghten test, which focused on the defendant's knowledge of the "nature and quality" of his act. Clark's contention was that he thought he was shooting an alien, not a police officer, and thus this part of the standard would have applied to his case.

The Supreme Court ruled that there was no constitutional requirement to include any specific language as part of an insanity defense. Nevertheless, the court did address conceptually the meaning of the phrase "nature and quality" of the act. The court agreed with the interpretation (e.g., Goldstein, 1967) that if indeed a defendant did not appreciate what he was doing, he would thus not be able to know that it was wrong, citing the language of the Arizona Court of Appeals: "It is difficult to imagine that a defendant who did not appreciate the 'nature and quality' of the act he committed would reasonably be able to perceive that the act was 'wrong' " (p. 350). Thus, the "nature and quality" prong was deemed not to add anything substantive to the insanity criteria, and its omission would therefore have no bearing on the verdict.

CASE LAW

Clark v. Arizona
(2006)

- The U.S. Supreme Court affirmed that there is no minimum standard that states must use to excuse mentally ill defendants from responsibility.

- The Court was willing to uphold a very restrictive approach toward expert mental health testimony as related to *mens rea* issues.

The other issue raised by Clark was not related to the insanity defense, but to his claim that he lacked the specific intent to kill a police officer (referred to in this case as the *mens rea* element). Clark was able to present lay testimony to address this issue, but he was barred from introducing mental health expert testimony. He claimed that it was an unconstitutional violation of his due process rights for the court to disallow expert mental health testimony on the impact of his schizophrenic disorder on his knowledge that the victim was a police officer, and on his ability to form the intent to kill a law enforcement officer (since this element was required for first-degree murder in this case). The Supreme Court ruled against him, stating that expert testimony on mental disorders could confuse the jury on the issue of the defendant's ability to form the intent, and therefore Arizona had justification to limit expert mental health testimony to the insanity defense, even if it barred such testimony from other issues, such as ability to form intent.

The Supreme Court did not specifically endorse the restrictive model, indicating that other states may choose to allow such testimony, but that Arizona's choice to limit expert mental health testimony was sensible and not violative of due process rights. Indeed, most other jurisdictions continue to allow such expert testimony, so that mental health professionals can explain to the trier of fact how an individual's mental status may have impacted on his ability to form the requisite intent. It is also notable that, even in Arizona, testimony relevant to the defendant's ability to form the requisite intent is allowed but restricted to lay, rather than expert, testimony.

Legal Procedures

The insanity defense is an affirmative defense, requiring the defendant to raise the issue. Differences exist across jurisdictions regarding the burden and standard of proof. Some jurisdictions place the burden on the state to prove that the defendant was sane, once the defense is raised. The standard can range from "preponderance of the evidence" (i.e., more likely than not), through "clear and convincing evidence," to the most stringent standard of "beyond a reasonable doubt." Other jurisdictions place the burden on the defense to prove insanity. The standards of proof in these states vary from "preponderance of the evidence" to "clear and convincing" evidence. It is useful for forensic clinicians to be aware of the standards and burdens of proof in the jurisdictions in which they practice, but it is not within the purview of the expert to opine on whether the particular standard of proof has been met. That is the responsibility of the trier of fact, which can be either a jury or a judge. This does not prevent the expert from commenting on the strength of the data forming the basis of the opinion and the degree of confidence in the opinion proffered.

Imposition of the Insanity Defense

Given the potential consequences of an insanity acquittal (psychiatric commitment for a lengthy period of time, including being subject to conditional release to the community), some defendants who appear to have a strong case may choose not to pursue it. In *Frendak v. U.S.* (1979), a Federal Court of Appeals ruled that a judge could not impose an insanity defense on a defendant who was competently choosing not to use that plea. The court noted that defendants may make this choice for rational reasons, including:

- not wanting to be subject to psychiatric commitment,
- not liking the conditions of confinement in a psychiatric hospital (preferring prison to a hospital),
- the stigma of being found insane,
- legal ramifications (including loss of right to vote in some states), or
- a desire to present their behavior in a political or religious context (rather than as related to a mental illness).

However, the court did allow imposition of an insanity defense in a situation in which the court determined that the defendant's decision to reject the plea was not made intelligently and voluntarily.

The decision about whether to impose a defense is made by the court at the time of trial. Thus, the forensic clinician may be required to conduct a CR evaluation prior to the issue being determined. Similarly, in some jurisdictions, the court can order a CR evaluation without the defense requesting it (although the defense may ultimately choose not to use the defense). The ethical and practical issues that emerge in these situations are discussed in Chapter 4.

Appointment of Forensic Evaluators

Forensic evaluators may be appointed by the court, or may be retained by either the prosecution or the defense. Although the nature of the evaluation should not vary based on the referral, there may be significantly different procedures and guidelines for communication of the results. Many jurisdictions have provisions for court-ordered evaluations to be conducted either by state (or federal) employees or by individuals or agencies under contract. A variety of models are utilized, including hospital-based and community-based (at the court, or at a correctional facility) evaluation systems (Grisso, Cocozza, Steadman, Fisher, & Greer, 1994). In these systems, the forensic evaluator's client is the court, and the procedures for disseminating the reports will vary. In some jurisdictions, the report will be sent directly to the court, the defense attorney, and the prosecution. In other states, the report is not shared with the prosecution unless the defense chooses to assert the insanity defense.

It is important for the forensic evaluator to understand at the outset who will be receiving the report and with whom the evaluator can communicate. This has important ramifications, because the nature of the CR evaluation necessitates a detailed inquiry and discussion with the defendant of her version of the alleged offense (see Chapter 5). As a consequence, the forensic evaluator, in many instances, obtains information from the defendant that could be considered a confession to a crime. This raises both constitutional (Fifth Amendment right against self-incrimination) and ethical issues that must be addressed. The information obtained during the CR evaluation cannot be introduced as evidence of guilt (other than to rebut a mental state defense). But, once the information is made available to the prosecution, secondary ramifications may arise in terms of prosecution strategy or ability to uncover other evidence.

WHEN THE EVALUATOR IS RETAINED BY THE PROSECUTION

Other issues may arise when the evaluator is hired by the prosecution. Typically, for a defendant to plead insanity, she must cooperate with an evaluation by an expert hired by the prosecution. Failure to cooperate can lead to the defendant being barred from asserting an insanity defense. If the defendant is unwilling to cooperate with the prosecution's expert, the evaluator should so inform the prosecutor and allow the attorneys and the court to determine how to proceed. The judicial decision about barring the defense in

such cases may take into consideration evidence that the defendant was "willfully" refusing to participate (as opposed to doing so, for example, in the context of paranoid delusions).

The evaluator hired by the prosecution should clarify with the retaining attorney the laws and procedures in the particular jurisdiction for disseminating information. The case of *Commonwealth v. Stroyny* (2002) highlights possible pitfalls. In that case, the prosecutor and a psychiatrist (hired by the prosecutor as a rebuttal expert to the defense's forensic expert) were chastised by the Appellate Court because the psychiatrist prematurely revealed to the prosecutor some of the defendant's statements obtained during the evaluation of CR. The court pointed out that, pursuant to Massachusetts case law, such statements made by a defendant could not be revealed to the prosecutor until such time as the court rules that privilege should be waived (typically, at the point at which the defense indicates that the defendant's statements, either through direct testimony, or through their own witness, will be introduced into evidence). This case is specific to Massachusetts; laws and procedures vary across states and the federal courts.

WHEN THE EVALUATOR IS RETAINED BY THE DEFENSE

Issues may arise as well even if the evaluator is retained by the defense. In many jurisdictions, if a forensic clinician is retained by the defense, information obtained during the CR evaluation is protected by attorney–client privilege. Under these circumstances, the information is provided only to the defense attorney, and it will be up to the attorney to release a report or call the expert to testify (*U.S. v. Alvarez*, 1975). However, other jurisdictions exempt these evaluations from the privilege. In the case of *Edney v. Smith* (1976) an Appellate Court upheld the constitutionality of the defense expert being subpoenaed to testify by the prosecution. That court concluded that "any possible prejudice may be balanced, within limits not exceeded in this case, by the strong counterbalancing interest of the State in accurate fact-finding by its courts" (p. 1054). This court, while recognizing the possible negative consequences to the defendant of having statements given to a defense-retained evaluator admitted into evidence by the prosecution, ruled that the interests of the state in obtaining a just outcome superseded the defendant's rights. Although in the *Edney* case there was no requirement that the defense-retained evaluator's report or opinion be released to the prosecution, once it was discovered, the prosecution was permitted to call the expert as a rebuttal witness.

These different approaches to the issue have yet to be resolved by the Supreme Court. Thus, each state can develop its own rules, and it is incumbent on forensic evaluators to ascertain, at the outset, the procedures followed in the particular jurisdiction in which they are practicing.

Forensic Mental Health Concepts

2

The central role of the forensic clinician in criminal responsibility (CR) evaluations is to obtain, and provide to the legal system, clinical data and analysis concerning the defendant's functioning, mental status, and capacities at the time of the alleged offense. The inquiry must seek data that are relevant for the legal definition of CR in the court's jurisdiction. Jurisdictions differ not only in the legal standard for insanity, but also in the terms used for the threshold question about mental condition—that is, whether the defendant had a "mental illness," "mental disease," "mental defect," or "mental retardation" at the time of the alleged offense. Furthermore, some jurisdictions may provide specific definitions for these terms, either in statute or case law, whereas others may not. The evaluator will always need to perform a thorough clinical evaluation, although the impairments that the evaluation reveals might differ in their legal effect in different jurisdictions. The clinician's task is to integrate all the data into a forensic formulation, consistent with local laws, regarding the functioning and mental status of the defendant at the time of the alleged offense.

As discussed in Chapter 1, most legal definitions of insanity have two main features: (a) a reference to mental disease or defect, and (b) a description of the specific incapacities that allow for acquittal by reason of insanity, if they existed at the time of the alleged offense as a consequence of the mental disorder. This chapter begins with a discussion of the relation between the law's "mental disease or defect" for purposes of insanity and the diagnostic conditions that are employed in clinical psychiatry and psychology. Then it explains concepts that have been developed in law and forensic practice that parallel the two main types of incapacities noted in legal standards for insanity: specifically "cognitive" incapacities and "volitional" incapacities. It is customary to refer to these as the two "prongs" of legal insanity standards.

The chapter then discusses special issues involved in considering conditions of intoxication at the time of the offense when interpreting the insanity standard. Finally, the chapter comments on conceptual issues associated with the legal definition of "diminished capacity."

Defining Mental Disorders in Insanity Evaluations

Regardless of their specific definitions of insanity, all jurisdictions require that a defendant asserting an insanity defense must show that he suffered from a "severe" disorder at the time of the alleged offense. Psychotic disorders (e.g., schizophrenia) and major affective disorders (e.g., major depression, bipolar disorder) are typically considered to meet this requirement of level of severity. It is noteworthy in this regard that the American Psychiatric Association (1983) proposed a definition that stated: "The terms mental disease or mental retardation include only those severely abnormal mental conditions that grossly and demonstrably impair a person's perception or understanding of reality . . . . " (p. 6). Although most successful insanity defenses involve a psychotic disorder, this does not mean that other disorders will not qualify an individual for consideration of an insanity defense. Rather, in such instances, it is necessary to demonstrate how the disorder was of such severity as to impair the defendant's ability to rationally perceive or understand the circumstances surrounding the alleged offense or to make rational choices.

Posttraumatic stress disorder (PTSD) is an example of a nonpsychotic

INFO

Most insanity defenses involve psychotic disorders and major affective disorders, but other disorders may also be considered in CR evaluations.

disorder that has sometimes been successfully used as part of an insanity defense. PTSD is listed as an anxiety disorder in the *Diagnostic and Statistical Manual of Mental Disorders, Fourth Edition, Text Revision* (*DSM-IV-TR*; American Psychiatric Association [APA], 2000), not as a psychotic disorder. For symptoms of this disorder to be relevant to an insanity defense, it is necessary to demonstrate that the defendant was experiencing acute symptoms at the time of the alleged offense that impaired her ability to realistically perceive the circumstances. Thus, a defendant might seek to demonstrate that she was experiencing a "flashback" at the time (i.e., that the defendant was reliving the trauma and believed that she was reexperiencing the original circumstances of the trauma, rather than appreciating present reality). This could suggest that the symptoms were of sufficient severity to offer a foundation for the insanity defense (Packer, 1983; Sparr & Atkinson, 1986).

Usefulness of Including a Formal Diagnosis in the Evaluation

Must the forensic evaluator always include formal diagnostic labels as part of the CR evaluation? Morse (1978) has argued that diagnoses are irrelevant, since they do not map directly onto the legal concepts. By contrast, the American Psychiatric Association's practice guidelines for conducting insanity evaluations (Giorgi-Guarnieri et al., 2002) recommend using a formal *DSM* or *International Classification of Diseases* (ICD) diagnosis, noting that "Most experts believe that a psychiatric diagnosis should be made whenever possible" (p. S26). In an empirical study of forensic examiners, Borum and Grisso (1996) found that a significant majority of both psychologists (almost 87%) and psychiatrists (93%) surveyed endorsed inclusion of a diagnosis as either an essential or recommended element in CR (insanity) reports.

Melton, Petrila, Poythress, and Slobogin (2007) offer a nuanced and balanced discussion of the rationale for including or excluding a formal diagnosis. They acknowledge that "a diagnosis, standing alone, is virtually useless to the legal system" (p. 259), but they identify several advantages to including a diagnosis in the

INFO

Advantages of Including a Formal Diagnosis

- Diagnostic categories are useful in gathering, evaluating, and organizing data

- Increases the credibility of the assessment

- Aids in determining whether a defendant's disorder is specifically excluded by legal standards in the jurisdiction

formulation. First, some jurisdictions specifically exclude certain diagnostic categories from qualifying for the insanity defense (such as drug or alcohol intoxication or antisocial personality disorder), so that a diagnostic label may be helpful in establishing whether the defendant's condition would even qualify for consideration of the defense. Second, the diagnostic labels may be useful to the attorneys involved, as a way of helping them determine the viability of the insanity claim.

The most significant argument offered by Melton and colleagues for the utility of including diagnoses, accompanied by a detailed description of the specific symptoms, is that certain diagnostic entities are more consistent with the severe level of pathology that is typically required for the insanity defense. Furthermore, it may be useful to consider the particular pattern of symptoms that typify certain diagnostic categories in order to assess whether the defendant's report is credible or is more likely a malingered or exaggerated presentation. For example, if a forensic evaluator documents that the defendant reported that she was responding to hallucinations at the time of the alleged offense, it will be helpful to the trier of fact if this is placed in context of what is known about psychiatric disorders. Did the defendant display other characteristics of schizophrenia, for example? Since the claim of hearing voices is self-reported, placing the symptom within a diagnostic category will likely aid in assessing the validity and significance of this symptom. By explaining that this woman has a history of being diagnosed with schizophrenia, and that this symptom is consistent with that diagnosis, the credibility of the assessment is enhanced.

A further argument for the utility of including specific diagnoses is that clinicians typically use diagnostic categories in order to gather, evaluate, and organize data. The types of questions asked and the information gathered are, to some extent, influenced by our understanding of diagnostic categories. For example, if a defendant claims to have no memory for the alleged offense, the clinician will consider several hypotheses, framed by an understanding of diagnostic entities. Does the defendant display signs of dementia? Was the defendant's memory impaired by acute intoxication, which led to registration amnesia? Does the defendant display other cognitive deficits?

Limitations of Formal Diagnoses in the Evaluation

2
chapter

These arguments point to the usefulness of including a diagnosis in the clinical formulation. But, it is important to recognize that the mere fact that an individual had a serious mental disorder at the time of the alleged offense is not enough to draw conclusions about insanity. Thus, one cannot assert that simply because the defendant suffered from bipolar disorder with mania, he was unable to control his behavior. Likewise, one cannot claim that the defendant was unable to appreciate the wrongfulness of his behavior simply because he is diagnosed with schizophrenia, paranoid type. Many people with these disorders are able to control their behaviors and appreciate wrongfulness much of the time. Identifying the diagnosis is important when the disorder frequently does impair reality testing or behavioral control. But whether or not it did have that effect at the time of the alleged offense requires more inquiry. Nevertheless, the diagnosis at least forms a threshold or foundation for further discussion of whether the symptoms exhibited impaired the capacities relevant to the insanity defense.

It is also important to keep in mind the caveat in *DSM-IV-TR* (APA, 2000) regarding the relationship between diagnoses and legal concepts. The introduction to the manual specifically refers to the use of the *DSM-IV* in forensic settings and states:

> When the *DSM-IV* categories, criteria, and textual descriptions are employed for forensic purposes, there are significant risks that

BEWARE
A formal diagnosis is not in itself sufficient to establish an insanity defense. The defendant's symptoms must have impaired her legally relevant capacities at the time of the alleged offense.

diagnostic information will be misused or misunderstood. These dangers arise because of the imperfect fit between the questions of ultimate concern to the law and the information contained in a clinical diagnosis. In most situations, the clinical diagnosis of a *DSM-IV* mental disorder is not sufficient to establish the existence for legal purpose of a "mental disorder," "mental disability," "mental disease," or "mental defect." (p. xxxii–xxxiii)

This caveat is intended to remind users of the *DSM* that the diagnoses are not *sufficient* for meeting the legal criteria; this does not mean that they are not useful as part of a comprehensive assessment of particular functional categories.

Mental Disease/Illness Versus Mental Defect

Many statutes refer not only to "mental disease" (or "mental illness"), but also "mental defect." The latter term is typically reserved for conditions such as mental retardation, development disabilities, and cognitive disorders (such as dementia) brought about by medical conditions or injuries to the brain. The relevant variable is the defendant's functional capacity (or incapacity) as related to the legal standard, not the particular diagnosis. Furthermore, for the purpose of the determination of CR, there is no legally significant difference between a "mental disease" and a "mental defect." Thus, one might debate whether an individual with Alzheimer's dementia should be considered to have a mental disease or a mental defect, but this point by itself would have no bearing on the issue of culpability.

INFO

Whether the cause of the defendant's incapacity is categorized as a "mental illness" or a "mental defect," the legal implications for CR are the same.

Defining the Cognitive Prong

All jurisdictions in the United States (except for New Hampshire, which uses the "product test" discussed in Chapter 1) define the incapacities that a mental disease or defect must have created at the time of the alleged offense in order to qualify for an insanity defense. Many jurisdictions refer to two broad types of incapacities, which are conventionally called the "cognitive" and "volitional" prongs of the definition of insanity. This section reviews the cognitive prong and how it has been conceptualized for purposes of guiding the forensic evaluation. The next section reviews the volitional prong.

The wording of the cognitive prong differs across states and the federal system; for example, "did not know the conduct was wrong," or "was unable to distinguish right from wrong," or was unable to "appreciate the wrongfulness of the conduct." But the common element involves an assessment of the defendant's capacity to recognize that the alleged behavior was wrong. There has been much discussion in the legal and professional literature, as well as in case law, regarding the meaning of "wrongfulness." Does it refer to deficits in the defendant's ability to understand that the act committed was "legally" wrong (that is, did the defendant know it was against the law)? Or, does it refer to the defendant's ability to understand that the act was "morally" wrong (that is, contrary to society's moral standards)?

The term "wrongfulness" was taken from the M'Naghten standard, but the discussions that accompanied the development of that standard were ambiguous, focusing sometimes on legal and at other times on moral standards. One of the confounding factors is that the framers took pains to point out that mere lack of knowledge of the law did not constitute insanity. However, they did not tackle the nuances of situations in which a defendant may understand that his act was illegal, but nonetheless believe that it was morally justified. It is noted that in the American Law Institute (ALI) standard, the word "criminality" is then modified by inclusion of the term "wrongfulness." The term "criminality" connotes a focus on whether the mental illness affected the individual's ability to understand that the behavior was illegal. The term "wrongfulness" in the ALI, as will be clear from the cases cited later, is generally understood to be a broader term, focusing on moral standards.

Moral Wrong Versus Legal Wrong

In jurisdictions applying the M'Naghten standard, the meaning of "wrong" is not as clear. In most cases, no meaningful distinction would exist between a legal and moral understanding. However, instances will occur in which the nature of a defendant's psychopathology is such that he retains knowledge that the behavior would result in legal sanctions, but he is convinced that the behavior is morally justified. Several cases, cited later, provide a sense of different courts' rulings and reasoning regarding the meaning of the term "wrong." In England, the preference has been for the narrower definition of "legal wrong," but in most cases in the United States, courts have opted for the definition to encompass "moral wrong."

CASE OF *NEW YORK V. SCHMIDT* (1915)

As far back as 1915 (*New York v. Schmidt*, 1915), Judge Cardozo of the New York Court of Appeals eloquently argued that the standard should include whether the defendant understood the act to be morally, as well as legally, wrong. In that case, Schmidt acknowledged that he knew that killing was against the law of the state, but claimed that he killed his female victim in response to the voice of God commanding him to do so as a sacrifice and atonement. The trial judge had instructed the jury that the relevant standard was whether the defendant understood that the act was against the law. The Appellate Court disagreed with this interpretation. Judge Cardozo wrote that using the narrow definition of legal wrongfulness would

> Rob the rule of all relation to the mental health and true capacity of the criminal. The interpretation placed upon the statute by the trial judge may be tested by its consequences. A mother kills her infant child to whom she has been devotedly attached. She knows the nature and quality of the act; she knows that the law condemns it; but she is inspired by an insane delusion that God has appeared to her and ordained the sacrifice. It seems a mockery to say that, within the meaning of the statute, she knows that the act is wrong . . . . We find nothing either in the history of the rule, or in its reason and purpose, or in judicial exposition of its meaning, to justify a conclusion so abhorrent. (p. 949)

This example is also known as the *deific decree* (i.e., the defendant believes that she has been commanded by God to act). Even some courts that have endorsed a narrow definition of wrongfulness have

INFO

In most U.S. jurisdictions, courts have defined "wrongfulness" to involve "moral wrong" as well as "legal wrong." The defendant may be found Not Guilty by Reason of Insanity (NGRI) if he believed his actions to be morally justified due to a delusion.

acknowledged this exception (e.g., *State v. Crenshaw*, 1983).

CASE OF *STATE V. HAMANN* (1979)

An opposing point of view was adopted by the Supreme Court of Iowa in *State v. Hamann* (1979). In that case, Hamann killed a man who worked with his father. Hamann maintained a delusional belief that his father's life was endangered by the victim, whom he characterized as a "malicious adversary." He acknowledged his understanding that killing the victim was a criminal act, but believed that society would recognize that he had "righted a great injustice." Hamann argued that the jury should have been instructed that the term "wrong" meant moral wrong, but the Iowa Supreme Court disagreed. They ruled that only impairment in understanding that an act was criminal should qualify a defendant for the insanity defense. They based their reasoning on concerns about the slipperiness of determining society's moral standards, arguing that established laws are the barometer of a society's moral standards. They wrote

> In this world of revolutionary and often violent change it is futile to pretend that our society maintains a consensus on moral questions beyond what it writes into its laws. Contemporary philosophers and theologians ponder mightily but without notable success to reach agreement on the "general mores" of our society. National debates rage over a myriad of moral issues. Few are resolved with anything approaching unanimity. Impossible uncertainty over the so-called general mores renders the appreciation of morality a tool unfit for the task of measuring sanity. (p. 183)

In establishing this ruling, the Iowa court recognized that it was in the minority, as most other jurisdictions had chosen to use the standard of moral wrong.

The majority of other courts that have addressed this issue have accepted the broader meaning of the term "wrongfulness." For instance, in *Wade v. U.S.* (1970), the Ninth Circuit Court of Appeals adopted the ALI standard for insanity in federal cases, saying:

> In approving the ALI formulation, we note that three Circuits have adopted the word "wrongfulness" (the ALI's suggested alternative) in place of "criminality" ' in order to exclude from the criminally responsible category those who, knowing an act to be criminal, committed it because of a delusion that the act was morally justified. We likewise believe that the term "wrongfulness" is preferable. (p. 72)

Subjective Versus Objective Standard

Even within the majority of jurisdictions that have adopted the moral wrongfulness standard, debate continues about yet another complicated issue: whether an "objective" or "subjective" standard of wrongfulness should be applied. As Goldstein and Rotter (1988) note, the distinction between these terms is whether the defendant's symptoms impaired her capacity to know that the acts committed would be considered wrong by society's standards of morality ("objective standard"), or whether the defendant, knowing that society would consider the acts wrong, nonetheless felt that that those acts were morally justified ("subjective standard").

The "subjective moral standard" is the most liberal or inclusive standard. In the majority of cases, the impact of the defendant's psychiatric symptoms will either impair (or not impair) the abilities related to both standards equally. However, there may indeed be cases in which there is a divergence between the standards. A number of appellate cases in the United States have focused on this distinction. Although no definitive ruling on this matter has been made (as it has not

INFO

Whether courts should apply an "objective standard" or "subjective standard" in assessing the cognitive prong has not yet been established in most jurisdictions.

been addressed by the U.S. Supreme Court and there are differences across jurisdictions), it is instructive to note how various courts have addressed this issue.

CASE OF *UNITED STATES V. SEGNA* (1977)

In *United States v. Segna* (1977), a case in the federal system, Joseph Segna was accused of shooting and killing a Native American policeman on a Navajo reservation. Although of Italian descent, Segna had reported to many people that he was a "persecuted Indian." He produced both lay and expert witnesses who corroborated the consistency of his reports of this delusion. Furthermore, the expert witnesses tied this delusional system to the shooting of the policeman and opined that, as a result, his ability to appreciate the wrongfulness of his behavior was impaired relative to the particular incident. Mr. Segna was nevertheless convicted, but his conviction was overturned on other grounds, not related to the issue of the cognitive prong. In remanding for a new trial, the Ninth Circuit Court of Appeals nevertheless chose to address the issue of the standard to be applied to determine appreciation of "wrongfulness."

At trial, Segna's lawyer had asked the judge to instruct the jury, regarding the definition of wrongfulness, that the term refers to moral wrongfulness rather than criminal wrongfulness. The trial judge did not agree to that definition, stating the term *moral* added nothing to the definition and would only result in confusion for the jurors. The Appeals Court disagreed, and provided a clear explanation of the possible meanings of the words *wrong* or *wrongfulness*:

> First, the word may mean legally wrong, or "contrary to law." Thus a person is criminally responsible if he has substantial capacity to appreciate that his act violates the law. Second, the word may mean "contrary to public morality." Here a person is criminally responsible, regardless of his appreciation of his act's legal wrongfulness, if he is aware at the time of the offending act that society morally condemns such acts. Third, the word may mean "contrary to one's own conscience." Under this "subjective" approach, the accused is not criminally responsible for his offending act if, because of mental disease or defect, he believes

that he is morally justified in his conduct—*even though* he may appreciate either that his act is criminal or that it is contrary to public morality. (p. 232, italics in original)

The Segna court concluded, consistent with its ruling in the Wade case, that the ALI standard clearly was intended to encompass moral wrongfulness and did not simply refer to an understanding that the act was prohibited by law. But, they acknowledged, there was less guidance on whether the term should be measured objectively or subjectively. This particular Court of Appeals decided that the subjective definition was preferable.

CASE OF *PEOPLE V. RITTGER* (1960)

Other courts, however, have ruled in the opposite direction, restricting the term to the objective meaning. In *People* v. *Rittger* (1960), Ronald Rittger, an inmate at Soledad prison, was charged with the murder of another inmate. The two men had previously fought but, at the time of the killing, the victim had not been threatening toward Rittger. Rittger claimed, however, that he was concerned that the victim might attack him at some point in the future; therefore, he felt that the homicide was committed in self-defense and was thus justified. Although there was conflicting testimony about whether Rittger was mentally ill, at least one psychiatrist testified that he was paranoid and suffered from schizophrenia, and that this was the basis for his fears about the victim. This psychiatrist further testified that, as a result of his experiences in prison, Rittger had developed a personal standard that the preemptive killing of the victim was justified.

The California Supreme Court, in reviewing this case, addressed the issue of how to interpret the word "wrong" (using the M'Naghten standard). The court noted that the defense psychiatrist's testimony was that Rittger was aware that his behavior was not in accordance with society's standards of right and wrong, but felt justified in his behavior based on his own standards, which were developed in the prison context. The Rittger court dismissed the subjective standard, writing

The fact a defendant claims and believes that his acts are justifiable according to his own distorted standards does not compel a finding of legal insanity. This is necessarily so if organized society is to formulate standards of conduct and responsibility deemed essential to its preservation or welfare, and to require compliance, within tolerances, with those standards. (p. 653)

In this case, the California Supreme Court clearly articulated the concern about using a subjective standard, since this would open the door to defendants claiming that their personal standards of morality justified their behavior. Although the rationale used for the contrary position, such as the Segna case, is that such subjective standards must be addressed in the context of a mental illness, the Rittger case demonstrates the limitations of that safeguard. It is clear from the court's discussion that not only did the opposing experts at trial disagree with the diagnosis, but the California Supreme Court, too, was skeptical about the basis for the conclusion that Rittger was mentally ill. Nonetheless, the Court noted that it was not within its purview to overrule the trier of fact. Thus, the variability among mental health professionals in diagnosing mental illness contributes to the conservative approach adopted by some courts in limiting the scope of the insanity defense by using an objective standard of wrongfulness.

CASE OF *PEOPLE V. STRESS* (1988)

Similarly, a California Appellate Court, in *People v. Stress* (1988) confirmed that "wrongfulness" referred to societal standards as opposed to "those standards peculiar to the accused" (p. 923). In this case, Stress had a long history of paranoia that included delusional beliefs involving a conspiracy including the government, media, and professional sports to prevent professional athletes from serving in the military. After years of failing to draw attention to this issue, he killed his wife with the intention of using the ensuing trial as a forum for his issues. A psychiatrist testified at his trial that Stress had committed the homicide to gain public attention to the issue, which he thought would save the lives of untold future generations. The testimony was that Stress' act was "necessary and right and would have been similarly seen so by the public at large if they knew the terrible secret truths that he knew" (p. 917). This last phrase clearly articulates the distinction between objective and subjective standards of wrongfulness. The Stress court ruled that when a defendant labors under a delusion that results in a belief that the behavior is morally justified, and would be so acknowledged by others if they had the relevant information, this (objective standard) constitutes substantial impairment in the cognitive prong of the insanity defense. This contrasts with the Rittger case, in which he understood that society would not agree that his behavior was justified, but was acting in accord with his own moral system.

Forensic Evaluator's Role in Relation to Differing Standards

The purpose of presenting these cases is not to try to assert any particular definition or precedent, but rather to highlight the issues involved in the legal system's approach to understanding the meaning of impairment in a defendant's understanding or appreciation that his behavior would be considered "wrong." In the majority of cases, the distinctions between legal and moral wrongfulness or between objective and subjective standards of morality will not be at issue. However, cases do exist in which there occurs a divergence between the standards (e.g., where the defendant may appreciate that the behavior is wrong from an objective standard but not from a subjective one). Forensic evaluators should then be cognizant of the distinctions in order to be able to present appropriate data to the court. In jurisdictions in which the legal definition has not been clearly articulated, it will not be within the purview of the forensic evaluator to determine whether such impairments meet the legal standard. However, the forensic evaluator can aid the court by explaining the defendant's particular symptoms and how they impact on the defendant's reality testing and capacity to reason regarding legal and moral standards.

> **BEST PRACTICE**
> Be familiar with the distinctions between legal and moral standards of "wrongfulness" and bring to the court's attention the defendant's relevant symptoms and impairments.

Defining the Volitional Prong

As noted in Chapter 1, significant controversy has surrounded the volitional prong: that is, the criteria related to impairment in ability to control one's criminal behavior. The American Psychiatric Association (1983) and the American Bar Association (1983) have argued that it cannot be reliably assessed. Morse (1994) has articulated his opposition to the volitional prong on philosophical and conceptual grounds, arguing that self-described "compulsions" represent difficult choices between conflicting forces (i.e., the pressure from the impulse to commit the wrongful act, and the competing pressure to avoid the negative consequences of the act).

This issue can be understood by referring to one of the examples cited by the Forensic Psychiatry guidelines for the insanity defense (Giorgi-Guarnieri et al., 2002) involving a defendant who they state *may* meet criteria for substantial impairment of the volitional prong. That hypothetical case involves a woman with an obsession that she is contaminated with germs, who disrobes outside her home for fear that she will contaminate the house. She is described as appreciating that public nudity is against the law (and, for the purpose of this discussion, would be considered wrong by society) but her "compulsion renders her unable to refrain from her behavior" (p. S29). Morse (1994), in addressing the issue of compulsions, argues that such a person may indeed fear very serious consequences from not acting on her compulsion, but is nonetheless *choosing* to accept the negative repercussions of violating the law.

This example also highlights the difficulty on a practical level of assessing the degree of *volitional impairment* that would be sufficient to excuse behavior. Even in the foregoing example, if one were to accept that the woman subjectively felt compelled to act, no external criteria exist for clinical evaluators to use to determine the degree of perceived compulsion. This analysis would apply to other disorders as well. For example, a defendant in the throes of a major depression may report experiencing dysphoria and hopelessness, and an "overpowering urge" to act on these feelings by killing her children and committing suicide (Rogers, 1987, p. 844). However, how is an evaluator to determine that the person's willpower was indeed overwhelmed, versus a formulation in which the person was in such great psychic pain that she chose to end the pain through a final, desperate act? There is no scientific basis for making such distinctions. Furthermore, no clinical benchmarks are available to determine what would *legally* be considered "substantial" impairment (Halleck, 1992).

Severe mania is another disorder often cited as best fitting the volitional prong (Giorgi-Guarnieri et al., 2002; Vitacco and Packer, 2004). Some individuals with mania report phenomenological experiences of racing thoughts (*DSM-IV-TR*, APA, 2000), which can impair their ability to reflect on their behavior and choose how to respond in a given situation. However, manic conditions differ in degree of severity, and it may be difficult to assess retrospectively how manic the defendant was at the time of the alleged offense. Furthermore, some individuals in a manic phase are characterized by increases in irritability, which may lower their inhibitions to act. Particularly with individuals who have a demonstrated history of impulsive behaviors even when not in a manic phase, assessing the degree of impairment attributable to the manic condition may be exceedingly difficult, if not impossible.

Criteria for Assessing Volitional Impairment

It is thus not surprising that the volitional prong is not only more controversial in terms of acceptance as a legal criteria, but more difficult for clinicians to assess in many cases. For instance, Warren, Murrie, Chauhan, and Morris (2004), reviewing over 5,000 insanity evaluations in Virginia over a 10-year period, found that of all defendants recommended as meeting insanity criteria, only 9% were deemed to meet the volitional prong only (compared to 44% who met cognitive criteria only, and 47% deemed to meet both the cognitive and volitional prongs). As noted in Chapter 1, only 16 states still maintain this element as part of their standard for the insanity defense. In those jurisdictions, the recommendations for criteria developed by Rogers

INFO

Rogers (1987) proposed five "representative criteria" for assessing volitional capacity:

1. capacity to make choices,

2. capacity for delay,

3. regard for apprehension,

4. forseeability and avoidability, and

5. result of a mental disorder.

(1987) would be helpful to consider: (a) capacity to make choices, (b) capacity for delay, (c) regard for apprehension, (d) forseeability and avoidability, and (e) result of a mental disorder. The last criterion is not specific to the volitional prong, but is incorporated into the threshold criterion, discussed earlier, of whether the individual suffered from a "diagnosable disorder of sufficient severity as to potentially impair volitional capacity" (Rogers, 1987, p. 848). If this question is answered affirmatively, then more detailed exploration of the other four criteria may be helpful in analyzing the data regarding the impact of the disorder on the defendant's volitional capacity, relative to the specific alleged offense.

chapter **2**

The fourth criterion (forseeability and avoidability) includes the following elements (Rogers, 1987, p. 848):

- Did the defendant choose to enter a high-risk situation in which he had prior difficulties with volitional control?

- Did the defendant anticipate that a loss of control was likely to occur based either on self-appraisal or on circumstances? If yes, what impact did this awareness have on subsequent behavior?

This criterion is conceptually distinguished from the first three, which will be discussed in more detail later. The first three criteria can be understood as a means to assess the degree of volitional control present at the time of the alleged offense. The criterion of forseeability/avoidability is related more to a judgment about the legal relevance of the loss of control. That is, even if the defendant did exhibit significant impairments in volitional control related to the specific acts that constitute the alleged offense, could he have taken steps earlier to minimize the risk of this occurring? Circumstances exist in which information about this issue should be obtained and provided to the court (for example, in cases of idiosyncratic intoxication or cases of delirium tremens, as discussed later). Whether or not to hold the defendant criminally responsible for such a decision is a moral/legal decision and not one that a clinician can make. Thus, the forensic evaluator does not have a basis for offering an opinion as to whether such a defendant meets the criteria for insanity.

For example, consider the hypothetical Mr. Doe, who has a long-standing diagnosis of schizophrenia, paranoid type. He functions well when engaged in treatment and taking his prescribed antipsychotic medications. However, when he discontinues his medication, his symptoms reemerge, and these have been associated in the past with assaultive behaviors. Mr. Doe does not like some of the side effects of his medications, so he discontinues them, experiences auditory hallucinations and paranoid delusions, and commits an assault and battery in reaction to these symptoms. A thorough forensic evaluation provides clear data that his relevant legal capacities were impaired. However, the prosecution argues that Mr. Doe discontinued his medication, knowing that this could lead to increased symptoms and an elevated risk for violence. This argument would be consistent with Rogers' fourth criteria. However, it would be inappropriate for a forensic evaluator to opine that this meant that Mr. Doe did not qualify for the volitional prong of the insanity defense because no specific legal criterion has been established to address this issue. Rather, the evaluator could provide information about the defendant's mental state at the time he discontinued his medications (i.e., was he psychiatrically stable at the time or had he already begun to experience symptoms that impacted his judgment), which the trier of fact could then decide how to apply.

The other three criteria (capacity to make choices, capacity for delay, regard for apprehension), which we will review next, can be used by evaluators to guide their interview questions, gathering of collateral data, and analysis of the data, in order to address the volitional prong. It should be noted that these criteria are not necessarily independent of each other, but rather represent different facets of behavior that can be attended to in the context of assessing the volitional prong. These are not meant to be quantified, but rather are "representative criteria" that direct inquiry and analysis.

CAPACITY TO MAKE CHOICES

The first factor directs attention to the defendant's ability to have made a choice to engage in the alleged behavior.

- Was the defendant capable of perceiving alternatives to the criminal behavior?

- Did the defendant believe that the only response to the situation was the specific criminal behavior, or did she consider alternatives?

- If alternatives were considered, what were they and what thought process did the defendant go through to choose the particular course of action?

- If no alternatives were considered, was there evidence that the defendant's ability to engage in deliberation was impaired?

- Was there any evidence that the defendant made any attempts to resist acting on the impulse?

- Was the criminal behavior part of goal-directed behavior aimed at accomplishing a specific outcome?

CAPACITY FOR DELAY

This factor directs the examiner's attention to the defendant's capacities or opportunities to stop the process of the alleged offense as it approached or occurred.

- Why did the defendant engage in the behavior at that specific time?

- Did the defendant choose the circumstances and place for the offense?

- Was there evidence that the defendant planned the actions or made preparations for them?

REGARD FOR APPREHENSION

This factor focuses on whether the defendant tried to avoid apprehension. The idea is that the defendant's efforts to avoid being caught would usually be inconsistent with the notion that the defendant was unable to regulate her behavior at the time of the alleged offense. (This dimension is also relevant to the cognitive prong, because it implies appreciation that the behavior was at least unlawful.)

- Did the defendant take actions, either prior to the act, and/or subsequent to it, to avoid detection and apprehension?

- What was the defendant's emotional reaction to having committed the act? Did she appear distressed?

These three factors are useful for deconstructing the concept of capacity to conform conduct at the time of the alleged offense. In different circumstances, any one of these factors may be more or less relevant to the specific facts of the case. It is also important to note that these factors provide guidelines to the evaluator, but are not dispositive regarding whether the defendant maintained or lacked substantial capacity to control the behavior. (For example, a delusional defendant may attempt to avoid apprehension by the police because she believes that the police are aliens intent on killing her.) Rather, these elements should be assessed in the context of the totality of the circumstances of the particular case. It is also important to assess these factors not only through the defendant's self-report, but also through use of collateral information, such as witnesses' descriptions of the defendant's behavior and demeanor.

The Role of Intoxication

Voluntary intoxication due to alcohol or drugs is not considered a basis for an insanity defense in U.S. jurisdictions, based on statutes and case law. The rationale for this exclusion, as expressed in *Kane v. U.S.* (1968), is that the mental disorder that impairs the legally relevant abilities "must have been brought about by circumstances beyond the control of the actor" (p. 735). Thus, even if a defendant's mental state is so impaired that she would otherwise meet the cognitive or volitional prong, if this mental condition was a function of intoxication, then it will not qualify the defendant to meet criteria for an insanity defense. The underlying legal and moral principle is

INFO

When it is determined that the defendant's impaired mental status is solely a function of acute intoxication, in all jurisdictions, the threshold criterion of mental disorder will not have been met.

that individuals should not be excused from the consequences that arise from voluntary consumption of drugs or alcohol.

The situation becomes more complex when the impairment is not due to acute intoxication but rather to

- the cumulative effects of intoxication (e.g., dementia or Korsakoff's psychosis),

- a psychotic disorder initiated by substance use, but continuing past the period of intoxication (e.g., substance-induced psychotic disorders, such as amphetamines, PCP, hallucinogens), or

- impairments brought about by cessation of substance use (such as delirium tremens).

As with the issue of "wrongfulness," the U.S. Supreme Court has not ruled on these issues, but the following discussion describes a number of cases in both state and federal courts that illustrate the legal analyses applied to these situations.

Intoxication and Fixed or Settled Insanity

A number of jurisdictions have distinguished long-term sequelae of substance abuse from the effects of acute intoxication (e.g., *State v. Hartfield*, 1990). The rationale employed in these circumstances is that if the defendant's criminal behavior was performed not in an intoxicated state, but rather resulted from a "fixed" or "settled" condition, the etiology of the defendant's mental disease or defect is irrelevant. Many jurisdictions thus allow long-term impairments like dementia to qualify for the insanity defense. The moral (as opposed to clinical) basis for this decision was eloquently articulated in a California Appeals Court case, *People v. Lim Dum Dong* (1938):

> There is, in truth, no injustice in holding a person responsible for his acts committed in a state of voluntary intoxication. It is a duty which every one owes to his fellow men, and to society, to say nothing of more solemn obligations, to preserve so far as lies in his power, the inestimable gift of reason. If it is perverted or destroyed by fixed disease, though brought on by his own vices, the law holds him not accountable, but if, by a voluntary act, he

temporarily casts off the restraints of reason and conscience, no wrong is done him if he is considered answerable for any injury which, in that state, he may do to others or to society. (p. 1038)

A counter-argument was articulated by the Colorado Supreme Court in the case of *Bieber v. People* (1993). That court also focused on the moral dimension, by which individuals are held accountable for ingesting substances that are known to cause impairment in reasoning, judgment, or behavior due to intoxication. The Bieber court stated that

We do not see any qualitative difference between a person who drinks or takes drugs knowing that he or she will be momentarily "mentally defective" as an immediate result, and one who drinks or takes drugs knowing that he or she may be "mentally defective" as an eventual, long-term result. In both cases, the person is aware of the possible consequences of his or her actions. (p. 816)

The Bieber court appears to be in the minority on this issue, as other courts have distinguished between intoxication and long-term sequelae of substance use (e.g., *People v. Conrad*, 1986; *Porreca v. State*, 1981).

SETTLED VERSUS FIXED INSANITY

Some courts have also recognized a concept of "settled" as opposed to "fixed" insanity. The latter term, as discussed above, refers to permanent damage brought about by substance use. The term "settled" refers to situations, such as drug-induced psychoses, in which the psychosis may have been triggered by substance use, but continues well beyond the point of intoxication, even if it is not permanent. A seminal case in this regard is *People v. Kelly* (1973), which exemplifies the issues involved in drug-induced psychoses. Valerie Kelly, an 18-year-old woman, was charged with assault with a deadly weapon for attacking her mother with kitchen knives. Expert testimony (by seven different psychiatrists) provided at her trial indicated that she reported hallucinations and delusions at the time of the assault, including thinking that she could communicate with her parents without actually speaking, and that her mother had told her that they "had devils," which made her realize that her parents were going to kill her. At her bench trial, the judge determined that indeed she could not understand that her act was wrong due to her psychotic state. However, the judge found her to be guilty, because the psychosis was brought about by her voluntary drug intoxication (LSD and mescaline, which she took between 50 and100 times in the months preceding the alleged offense, with the last use being the day before) and was not "permanent." The California Supreme Court overturned the conviction, ruling that Kelly met criteria for legal insanity. The Court ruled that the psychosis need not be permanent, but rather "settled," meaning that the psychosis continued past the period of intoxication (in this case there was evidence that the psychosis lasted many months beyond the last use of drugs).

2
chapter

This distinction has been accepted by other courts as well. In *Parker v. State*, 1969), the court dealt with the issue by describing two categories; the first category is when the defendant's behavior occurs during a period of acute intoxication and the second category involves situations in which the intoxication resulted in longer-term impairments. They articulated the difference as follows:

> If a person drinks intoxicating liquor and is sane both prior to drinking and after the influences of the intoxicant has worn off, but is insane by the applicable test while under the influence of the intoxicant, he comes under the first category. If he is insane whether or not he is directly under the influence of an intoxicant, even though that insanity was caused by voluntary drinking, he comes under the second category. (p. 388)

This is a useful heuristic for distinguishing the effects of intoxication. It should be noted that being intoxicated, in these jurisdictions, does not automatically exclude an insanity defense, if it can be proved that the impaired mental state was not limited to the period of acute intoxication.

CASE LAW
People v. Kelly
(1973)

● The defendant could not understand the wrongfulness of her act due to a psychosis that was brought about by drug use.

● California Supreme Court ruled that the psychosis need not be permanent but only "settled," that is, continuing beyond the point of intoxication.

Involuntary/Pathological Intoxication

As noted earlier, the rationale for barring defendants from using acute intoxication as a basis for an insanity defense is that defendants are held legally responsible for the consequences of voluntary substance use. However, courts have shown more flexibility when unusual circumstances exist regarding the anticipated or foreseeable consequences of the substance use. The most clear-cut example involves involuntary intoxication, which can result either from an individual unknowingly ingesting a substance (e.g., not being aware that a drink was "spiked") or from a reaction to a legally prescribed medication. In such instances, the exclusion of intoxicated states from the insanity defense would not apply.

A more complicated situation involves an idiosyncratic or pathological reaction to alcohol. This can happen when the defendant's mental status was severely impaired in reaction to imbibing a small amount of alcohol that would not otherwise be expected to cause intoxication. The ALI Model Penal Code (MPC; ALI, 1985) includes a provision for use of pathological intoxication as a basis for an insanity defense if the cognitive or volitional prong is met. The term is defined (2.08[4]) as "intoxication grossly excessive in degree, given the amount of intoxicant, to which the actor does not know he is susceptible."

In *Kane v. U.S.* (1968), a Federal Court of Appeals focused on the issue of the defendant's knowledge of his susceptibility. In that particular case, the Court determined that the defendant was aware of his lower tolerance for alcohol and the impact on his behavior, and thus would not have met the ALI criteria. It should be noted that the *Kane* court did not rule on the admissibility of pathological intoxication as a defense. Rather, the court pointed to the defendant's knowledge of the consequences to determine that the issue was moot. This issue has not been legally resolved and is open to interpretation across jurisdictions. However, even if it is accepted as a defense, it is likely to be available only once—the first time a defendant has such a reaction. Further instances are likely to be excluded on the grounds that the defendant was aware of the susceptibility and chose to drink anyway.

Withdrawal Effects

A similar analysis applies to impairments caused by withdrawal from substance use. Individuals undergoing substance withdrawal delirium (from alcohol, sedative, hypnotic, or anxiolytic drugs) may experience significant distortions in reality testing, such as disorientation, hallucinations, or misperceptions. For instance, an individual experiencing such delirium may hallucinate that people are hovering over her or may interpret a loud sound as a gunshot (*DSM-IV-TR*, APA, 2000, p. 137) and may react violently. In such situations, a determination may be made that, as a result of the delirium, the individual's abilities were impaired on either or both the cognitive and volitional prongs of the insanity defense. This level of impairment may be considered not an effect of intoxication, but an effect of cessation of intoxication, and thus not subject to exclusion from the insanity defense. Furthermore, unlike acute effects of inebriation, symptoms of delirium are not an anticipated consequence of substance use. However, as with pathological intoxication, an individual who has had repeated episodes of delirium associated with withdrawal is not as likely to prevail with an insanity defense, since she would likely have an expectation of such effects (e.g. *People v. Toner*, 1922).

INFO

The clinical information and formulation that are relevant for the court include

- whether the behavior can be attributed primarily to a preexisting psychotic disorder that was exacerbated by substance abuse,

- whether the behavior can be attributed to a psychotic disorder that was induced by substance use but continued beyond the period of intoxication,

- whether the alleged criminal behavior can be attributed primarily to the effects of acute intoxication,

- whether the impaired mental state was an atypical reaction to the use of alcohol or drugs, or

- whether the defendant has had previous instances of impairment related to the alcohol or substance use.

As with the earlier discussion about the differing legal interpretations of "wrongfulness," forensic evaluators must be cognizant of the distinctions between the clinical analysis and the legal determination of when an individual will be excused from the consequences brought about by alcohol or substance use. However, clinicians must be aware of the legal concepts, in order to be able to provide relevant information to the court.

Diminished Capacity

As noted in Chapter 1, diminished capacity is limited to a determination of the defendant's ability to form the requisite specific intent that is an element of the offense charged. A defendant who may qualify for the insanity defense on the grounds that he killed a stranger because he thought this man was part of a conspiracy to kill him would nevertheless be considered to have formed the intent to kill. The distortions in perception, or impairments in volitional control, that form the basis of an insanity defense are likely to be irrelevant to whether a defendant was able to form the intent to commit the act. In this example, the defendant intended to kill the victim, albeit for irrational motives. As Clark (1999) and Morse (1979) have articulated, very few circumstances would result in an inability or incapacity to form an intent. Clark (1999) suggested very rare examples, including a defendant suffering from a seizure or a profoundly retarded individual who could not comprehend the concept of stealing. However, for the vast majority of cases, the presence of psychopathology is not likely to result in loss of capacity to engage in intentional behavior.

In other cases, the defendant is not asserting *incapacity* to form intent, but rather claims not to have formed the intent. The case of *Clark v. Arizona* (2006) discussed in Chapter 1 is an excellent example of this point. Clark claimed that he thought the person he shot and killed was an alien, and therefore that he did not form the intent to shoot a police officer (which was an element of the crime). No claim was made that he was incapable of intending to shoot an officer, but only that in the specific case, he did not form that intent. Had his experts been allowed to testify, they could have explained that Clark's claim was consistent with his delusional beliefs, which are a common symptom of schizophrenia. However, it would not be proper for a forensic evaluator to opine as to whether indeed the defendant formed the intent; this is the factual issue that the jury must decide.

Limits on Mental Health Testimony

A number of jurisdictions have enacted legislation or adopted case law to limit expert mental health testimony on diminished capacity. Arizona, for example, has simply prohibited any mental health testimony on this issue (as discussed in the Clark case). Other states have limited diminished capacity to homicide cases, to address issues of whether the defendant premeditated the act. In these cases, forensic clinicians may be able to provide data and analysis that are consistent with a defendant's claims that the act was impulsive and not planned; however, the expert would not be able to state that the defendant was incapable of premeditating or did not in fact premeditate. Some jurisdictions, including the federal system, have incorporated this distinction into formal rules or statutes. For example, the Federal Rules of Evidence were modified in 1984 to specifically state that

> No expert witness testifying with respect to the mental state or condition of a defendant in a criminal case may state an opinion or inference as to whether the defendant did or did not have the mental state or condition constituting an element of the crime charged or of a defense thereto. (Federal Rules of Evidence, 704[b]).

Intoxication and Diminished Capacity

The issue of intoxication and its relevance to diminished capacity is subject to significantly different conceptualizations. Some states have adopted the same rationale as used for the insanity defense; the defendant should be held responsible for all behaviors that occur as a result of the voluntary ingestion of alcohol or drugs. However, other jurisdictions have determined that it is the responsibility of the state to prove all of the elements of a crime, and thus defendants have due process rights to produce evidence to rebut the claim that a particular intent was present, even if the lack of intent was due to intoxication.

The U.S. Supreme Court reviewed this issue in the case of *Montana v. Egelhoff* (1996). Egelhoff had been found in a car by police, with two victims who had each been killed by a single gunshot to the head. An hour later, Egelhoff's blood alcohol level was 0.36. He was charged with deliberate homicide, which entailed the elements of knowingly and purposely causing the victims' death. At his trial, he attempted to argue that his ability to act knowingly and purposely was impaired by his extreme intoxication, but was barred from doing so by a Montana law that explicitly barred consideration of intoxication in negating a required element of a crime. The U.S. Supreme Court upheld his conviction. Although the Court recognized that a number of states had found a constitutional right to present such evidence, they ruled that this was not a fundamental principle and that Montana had legitimate interests in developing a law that prohibited consideration of intoxication. Thus, the Court left it up to each jurisdiction to decide whether or not intoxication could negate specific intent; a majority of states still allow this use (Goldstein, Morse, & Shapiro, 2003).

Even in jurisdictions that allow such testimony, the applicability of clinical expertise is likely to be very limited (Clark, 1999). Elevated blood alcohol levels and even evidence of an alcoholic blackout are useful data, but are not determinative of a defendant's ability to form the requisite intent. "Blackouts" represent periods of time in which memory was not encoded and thus help explain why the individual may genuinely have no recoverable memory of the time period involved. However, individuals experiencing such conditions are not necessarily impaired in their ability to engage in intentional behavior; indeed, one of the hallmarks of blackouts is that the individual does not remember afterward engaging in behaviors that appeared quite organized and purposeful. The applicability of clinical expertise regarding the effects of intoxication may more likely be relevant to situations in which the defendant claims to have acted impulsively and not in a premeditated manner; however, at the most, the clinical data could be considered *consistent* with such a claim, but not dispositive.

BEWARE Clinical data regarding level of intoxication are not determinative of a defendant's diminished capacity to form intent.

Even when there are clear data regarding a high level of intoxication, forensic evaluators should be cautious about offering opinions that a defendant's capabilities were impaired, in the face of clear behavioral data indicating intent. This author was involved in a case in which the defendant had a blood alcohol level above 0.30 and had also been using a variety of illicit drugs. He stumbled into a gas station, brandished a rifle, announced, "This is an armed robbery," and demanded that the clerk give him the larger bills that were kept under the cash drawer. He took the money, went home, and awoke the next morning reportedly with no memory of the robbery. His attorney attempted to claim that his level of intoxication was so high that he could not possibly have formed the intent to commit the robbery. However, his actions and overt statements at the time belied such a claim. Analyses of whether or not a particular defendant had the "capacity" to form a particular intent are moot when there is evidence that the intent was indeed formed.

Extreme Emotional Disturbance

Cases involving extreme emotional disturbance (EED) place similar limitations on the forensic evaluator's opinions. In cases in which EED is based on a mental abnormality, forensic evaluators can be very helpful to the court in describing the defendant's mental condition and how it impacted his behavioral controls and ability to think and act rationally. However, as Kirschner and colleagues (2004) discuss, the legal standard is whether the defendant's behavior can be *reasonably* explained, a judgment which must be made by the trier of fact. They argue that

> While mental health professionals may be qualified to express an opinion as to the nature of a defendant's emotions at the time of a crime, the remaining question is whether mental health professionals have any special expertise in determining when an extreme emotional response to a situation is "reasonable." We believe they do not. (p. 130)

EED cases are a good example of the relationship between clinical data and legal determinations; the forensic evaluator can aid the

BEWARE It is the evaluator's role to provide useful clinical information and formulations to the court, not to determine whether the defendant's actions should be considered reasonable.

court by providing a good clinical formulation, incorporating specialized knowledge about mental disorders and human behavior. However, the determination of whether the defendant's reaction should be considered reasonable is a moral and legal decision that exceeds the role boundaries of the forensic professional.

Empirical Foundations and Limits | **3**

Research on criminal responsibility (CR) has been relatively limited, despite the important role that CR evaluations have played in the history of forensic psychology and psychiatry. Studies tend to have focused on the characteristics of cases in which the insanity defense is raised, with far less emphasis on the nature of CR evaluations. This chapter reviews research in those areas.

Correlates of Acquittal by Reason of Insanity

A number of studies have examined characteristics associated with a successful insanity defense. Melton and colleagues (2007) summarized results of studies conducted from 1967 to 1985 in Michigan, New York, California, and Georgia. In those studies, the percentage of insanity acquittees with a diagnosis of a psychotic disorder ranged from 68% to 97%. These studies, however, did not compare insanity acquittees to defendants who were convicted. Boehnert (1989) compared 30 male defendants in Florida who were found Not Guilty by Reason of Insanity (NGRI) with 30 men, matched on crime, who were unsuccessful in the use of the insanity defense, having been found guilty and imprisoned. The insanity acquittees were more likely to have been previously found Incompetent to Stand Trial (80% vs. 30%). Although formal diagnoses were not reported, Boehnert noted that 28 of the 30 insanity acquittees had a severe axis I disorder, whereas 23 of the 30 convicted men appeared "less psychotic" (p. 38).

Packer (1987) compared 50 homicide defendants in Michigan (1980–1983) who were acquitted by reason of insanity (NGRI) with a randomly selected (within gender) group of homicide defendants evaluated for insanity but convicted (Guilty). Consistent with Boehnert's data, the NGRI group was significantly more likely to have been found Incompetent to Stand Trial (68%) than the Guilty group (14%). Significant differences were also found in previous conviction for a felony (NGRI 16% vs. 50% for the Guilty group), prior psychiatric hospitalization (62% vs. 22%), and diagnosis of a psychotic disorder (82% vs. 14%).

Callahan, Steadman, McGreevey, and Clark-Robbins (1991) collected data across eight states and found that 84% of those acquitted by reason of insanity had received a diagnosis of "schizophrenia or another major mental illness (other psychotic or affective disorder)" (p. 336). Cochrane, Grisso, and Frederick (2001), using a large database of defendants (1,710 individuals) referred for evaluations of competence to stand trial and criminal responsibility in federal courts, likewise found that those with a diagnosis of psychosis had the highest likelihood of being adjudicated NGRI. Reviewing a sample of defendants evaluated over a 10-year period in Virginia, researchers Warren, Murrie, Chauhan, and Morris (2004) found that 65% of defendants recommended as NGRI had received a diagnosis of psychosis (as contrasted with only 26% of those recommended as sane). In that study, prior psychiatric hospitalization and *not* being under the influence of substances at the time of the offense were also found to be significantly related to the recommendation for a finding of NGRI.

Although these studies do not represent a systematically thorough inquiry into the insanity defense in the United States, taken in aggregate they suggest that individuals who are found insane are likely to be diagnosed with a psychotic disorder. This does not mean that such a diagnosis is required for an insanity defense. However, it belies the public perception (Chapter 1) that the insanity defense is used capriciously.

The Quality of Criminal Responsibility Reports

A limited empirical literature exists on examiners' CR reports. That literature includes evaluations of the quality of reports, as well as surveys of experienced forensic psychologists and psychiatrists regarding the matters that should be included in CR reports.

One of the earliest studies to evaluate CR reports was conducted in Michigan by Petrella and Poythress (1983), who sent actual reports by forensic psychologists, psychiatrists, and social workers to judges and lawyers to review. Their study included both competence to stand trial reports and CR reports, but it focused only on comparing psychologists to psychiatrists (and found little difference between them in various indices of quality). This study was conducted at a time when CR evaluations were conducted predominantly by psychiatrists, and it demonstrated that these evaluations could be performed at the same level of quality by psychologists. Given that there were only two raters, this study did not provide information about the *absolute* quality of the reports (on a 9-point scale, the judge rated the reports, on average at 4.75, slightly above the median, whereas the lawyer's average rating was 7.05). However, additional information from this study was provided in a subsequent publication (Melton et al., 2007, p. 586) that offered some insight into qualitative issues that are relevant to legal professionals, but which may not be as apparent to the clinicians. In particular, the legal professionals labeled as unclear a number of terms that are used routinely by forensic evaluators, such as "delusional ideation," "affect," "lability," "loosening of associations," and "oriented to time, place, and person." The implication for report writing will be discussed in Chapter 7.

Studies Indicating Problems With Adequacy of Information

Other studies across a number of jurisdictions have suggested more significant problems with CR reports. Heilbrun and Collins (1995) reviewed reports conducted in Florida in both a hospital (167 reports) and community setting (110 reports). Their study included both competence to stand trial and CR reports and focused on the presence or absence of certain types of information in the reports (as opposed to a qualitative assessment). Several findings raised concerns about examiners' CR reports.

First, although 97% of inpatient CR reports indicated that the defendant was informed of the purpose of the interview, this was true for only 30% of the CR reports performed in the community— that is, outside inpatient (hospital) settings. It could not be determined whether the community evaluators failed to notify the defendants or just failed to document the notification, but, either way, this omission was considered a source of concern.

Second, results from prior mental health evaluations were included in 70% of inpatient CR reports but in only about one-third of the community-based reports. "Other" sources of information were cited in only 33% of CR evaluations and 46% of evaluations that combined CR with competence to stand trial. Finally, only about one-half of CR reports actually provided discussions of how the results were related to the various components of the statutory definition of insanity (as Florida uses a M'Naghten standard, these included knowing "what he/she was doing," the "consequences" of the behavior, and knowing if the behavior "was wrong"). When reports in which the evaluator cited lack of adequate information to allow a conclusion were excluded, the percent addressing these three components were 56%, 37%, and 41%, respectively.

Other studies have also raised concerns about the adequacy of information provided in CR reports. Reviewing forensic reports in Florida, researchers Otto, Barnes, and Jacobson (1996) found that of 71 CR reports, only 10% obtained data from third party sources in addition to the defendant' self-report. Warren, Murrie, Chauhan, Dietz, and Morris (2004) reported on a large sample (5,171) of reports in Virginia, performed over a 10-year period. They found that "Evaluators often offered their opinions on the basis of incomplete data" (p. 183). Specifically, in over one-half of the cases, opinions on insanity were offered in the absence of a review of statements made by the defendant, witness statements, or the defendant's criminal record. System variables may have contributed to the evaluators not obtaining these data, but it is troubling nevertheless that 22% of the psychiatrists and 14% of the psychologists offered opinions on the issue of sanity without having reviewed information about the alleged offense.

More encouraging data were provided from Massachusetts, a state with a comprehensive training program for public-sector forensic psychologists and psychiatrists (Fein et al., 1991). In that jurisdiction, three experienced forensic evaluators (two psychologists and one psychiatrist) blindly reviewed a total of 102 CR reports. Based on consensus ratings, 80% of the reports were considered to have documented sufficient data relevant to the CR issue. Furthermore, 72% of the reports were judged to have provided clear reasoning for the conclusions offered (Packer & Leavitt, 1998).

Summary of Data on Quality of Evaluations and Reports

In summary, we have very limited data regarding the quality of (or deficiencies in) CR evaluations and reports among forensic clinicians in the U.S. This is remarkable in that there are far more studies of the quality of competence to stand trial reports (e.g., Nicholson & Norwood, 2000), which are often produced by the same clinicians who conduct CR evaluations. The data that are available, which indicate deficiencies in the quality of services being provided, most likely reflect lack of adequate training of forensic evaluators in those jurisdictions (Packer, 2008). Only the data from Packer and Leavitt (1998), which is limited to one state in which there is extensive continuing education for forensic clinicians, can be considered to be indicative of the ability of properly trained clinicians. Further research, across jurisdictions, would seem to be important for improving the training of examiners who perform CR evaluations. Such research should use as a foundation what experienced forensic clinicians

INFO

Limited data are available on the quality of CR evaluations and reports, although many of the studies that have been completed indicate a need for improved training.

believe are important elements of CR evaluations. Fortunately, some research is available to provide that information.

Clinicians' Opinions About Standards of Practice for Criminal Responsibility Evaluations

In the most comprehensive study of forensic clinicians' opinions about standards of practice for CR evaluations, Borum and Grisso (1996) surveyed a group of forensic psychologists (53) and psychiatrists (43) who were either board certified or who had at least 5 years of forensic experience. (Their study also included competence to stand trial, but only the CR data are reported here.) Respondents were asked to rate the importance of a number of components in CR reports, as either essential, recommended, optional, or contraindicated. The authors considered 70% endorsement to be an indicator of consensus among forensic clinicians about the importance (or lack of importance) of various elements of CR reports.

Identifying Information

Regarding the information that identifies the case early in the report, consensus existed among both the psychologists and psychiatrists that certain elements were "essential" for inclusion in a CR report (Table 3.1). Although not quite meeting the criteria for consensus established by the authors, 70% of psychiatrists and 60% of psychologists endorsed that it was essential to indicate that the defendant was informed of the limits of confidentiality and privilege.

There were several items regarding basic identifying information that were not perceived as essential by forensic evaluators in this study. Among these items was documentation of an attempt to contact the defense attorney and assessing the defendant's understanding of the purpose of the evaluation. No explanation is given for the opinions on these issues, as the survey did not provide an opportunity for follow-up. The variety of circumstances in which the respondents worked could have influenced their responses to these items. For example, no distinction was made in the survey question about whether the referral came from the defense attorney, the prosecutor, or the court. The importance of these issues may

Table 3.1 | Essential Elements of a Criminal Responsibility Report: Identifying Information

- Basic identifiers of the defendant (name, data of birth)

- Referral source: identifying whether the report was requested by one of the attorneys or the court

- Report date

- Charges: listing the formal criminal charges (and dates on which they allegedly occurred) which were the focus of the criminal responsibility evaluation

- A statement of the purpose of the evaluation

- Identification of the location and date(s) of the interviews

- Listing of other sources of information (collateral contacts, records, police reports, testing)

- Documentation of disclosure to the defendant of the purpose of the evaluation

(*Source*: Borum, R., & Grisso, T. (1996). Establishing standards for criminal forensic reports: An empirical analysis. *Bulletin of the American Academy of Psychiatry and the Law, 24*, 297–317.)

depend not only on the circumstances under which the evaluator was retained (i.e., hired by defense, prosecution, or appointed by the court), but also on the procedures regarding to whom the report is released (as discussed in Chapter 1, "Legal Procedures").

Data

The evaluators in this survey believed that certain types of data were essential in a CR report (Table 3.2).

Several other data elements were at least "recommended" by over 70% of each group but did not achieve the level of consensus required to be considered "essential." One was medical history: approximately 64% of each group recommended this as an essential

Table 3.2 | Essential Types of Data in a Criminal Responsibility Report

---

- Psychiatric history: information about the defendant's history of mental illness or mental retardation

- Mental health records: an indication that records were reviewed or at least attempts were made to procure such records

- Current mental status: includes both a description of the defendant's mental state at the time of the interview (e.g., thought process, thought content, level of intellectual functioning) as well as a formal mental status exam

- Information obtained from the police report about the defendant's behavior at the time of arrest

- Statement about the defendant's use (presence or absence) of psychotropic medications at the time of the evaluation and in the period since the arrest

- Information about alcohol and/or substance abuse prior to the time of the alleged offense

- Defendant's disclosure: information obtained from the defendant about his behavior at the time of the alleged offense (or a statement that the examiner attempted to obtain the information but the defendant was unable or unwilling to provide such an account)

(*Source:* Borum, R., & Grisso, T. (1996). Establishing standards for criminal forensic reports: An empirical analysis. *Bulletin of the American Academy of Psychiatry and the Law, 24,* 297–317.)

element. Documentation of prior diagnoses was endorsed as "essential" by 73% of the psychiatrists and 66% of the psychologists. A third element that was "recommended" by over 90% of each group, but did not reach the 70% level for being considered "essential," was collateral description of the alleged offense (obtaining information from witnesses or others who encountered the defendant around the time of the alleged offense). Given the significant emphasis in the literature on this element of forensic evaluations (e.g., Heilbrun, Warren & Picarello, 2003), it is not clear why this component was not rated as essential by a higher percentage. Nevertheless, it is noteworthy that almost all respondents identified it as at least "recommended."

Two other components were not considered essential by even a majority of either group: current status in other settings (such as hospital or jail), and psychological testing. Fewer than 30% of the psychologists and only 16% of the psychiatrists deemed psychological testing as essential. (The rationale for use of psychological testing in CR evaluations will be discussed in Chapter 5.)

Opinions

Finally, considerable divergence was seen in clinicians' opinions about elements of the "Opinions" section of the report—the section that interprets the data and arrives at a conclusion about the defendant's capacities related to the legal standard for insanity. Consensus existed among both psychiatrists and psychologists concerning the "essential" nature of only two elements:

- an opinion about the presence or absence of mental illness (although there was lack of consensus as to whether the report should address whether such a mental illness met the legal criteria of "mental disease or defect," with about one-third of the sample deeming this essential, but between 20% and 30% indicating that an opinion about the legal criteria was contraindicated); and

- an opinion as to the degree to which a defendant's mental illness did or did not influence the capacities relevant to the legal determination of criminal responsibility.

Psychiatrists tended to place more emphasis on the need to include a formal diagnosis (74% vs. 61% for psychologists, although in total 90% of psychologists agreed that this was at least "recommended"). Over 85% of the respondents agreed that providing a rationale for how the examiner arrived at an opinion on mental illness, and for the relationship between the mental illness and the CR issue, was either recommended or essential. Almost 60% of the psychiatrists, but only 40% of the psychologists, endorsed the inclusion of an *ultimate issue opinion*, whereas almost 20% of each group thought that an ultimate issue opinion was contraindicated.

The latter results highlight the lack of consensus in the field regarding the matter of ultimate issue opinions (which will be discussed in more depth in Chapter 7). It should be noted, however, that respondents may have differed in their interpretations of what constituted an ultimate issue opinion. Some may have considered an ultimate issue opinion a statement that the defendant "met (or did not meet) criteria for legal insanity," whereas others may have considered even a statement that the defendant "demonstrated substantial lack of capacity to appreciate the wrongfulness of her behavior" as indicative of an ultimate issue opinion.

These data provide useful guidance about some of the most important elements of CR reports, particularly those for which consensus existed among both disciplines. However, given the variety of settings in which the respondents worked and the lack of opportunity to assess their rationales, the significance of those areas in which there were differences of opinion is not clear. Nevertheless, it is striking that for most of the domains, there was agreement both within and between psychology and psychiatry about what constitutes good practice in CR reports.

The Use of Structured Tools in Criminal Responsibility Evaluations

Limited research has examined the use of standardized, structured assessment methods in CR evaluations. Some have focused on general psychological tests and others on *forensic assessment instruments* (FAIs) that collect data specific to the forensic questions involved in CR evaluations.

Psychological Testing

In a survey by Borum and Grisso (1995), two-thirds of forensic psychologists and psychiatrists deemed psychological testing as "recommended" or "essential" in CR evaluations (but only a small minority considered it essential). As part of their study, Borum and Grisso asked the respondents more detailed questions about psychological testing. Among the forensic psychologists, 57% reported using tests almost always (defined as more than 80% of the time) in CR evaluations, and 11% reported frequent use (41–80%). Of the 43 psychiatrists, only 28% reported that they incorporated testing into their reports almost always, and 14% reported frequent use.

Respondents who reported using tests at least occasionally were also asked to identify specific instruments. Among the 50 psychologists who identified specific tests, 94% reported using the Minnesota Multiphasic Personality Inventory (MMPI) and 78% reported using the Wechsler Adult Intelligence Scale (WAIS), but only 32% reported use of the Rorschach test. Borum and Grisso concluded that the results do not support a standard requiring psychological testing in every CR case, but do suggest that testing is the norm, rather than the exception, and that "psychologists ought to be held accountable to explain why they have *not* used psychological testing" (p. 471) in a CR case in which testing was not employed.

In a more recent study, Lally (2003) surveyed all psychologists who were listed as diplomates in forensic psychology by the American Board of Professional Psychology (ABPP). Sixty-four psychologists responded to the survey, which inquired about their opinion as to whether particular psychological tests and instruments were "unacceptable," "acceptable," or "recommended" for CR evaluations. The only two tests that more than half of the respondents "recommended" for CR evaluations were the MMPI-2 and the WAIS-III. Tests that were rated by more than half the forensic psychologists as acceptable for this type of evaluation included the Personality Assessment Instrument (PAI), Millon Clinical Multiaxial Inventory-III (MCMI-III), Stanford-Binet Revised, and neuropsychological batteries (Halstead-Reitan and Luria-Nebraska). Projective drawings, Thematic Apperception

Test (TAT), and sentence completion were categorized as unacceptable (meaning that at least half the respondents rated it so), and the Rorschach test was deemed to be equivocal.

Archer, Buffington-Vollum, Stredny, and Handel (2006) surveyed a broader group of psychologists, including not only those board certified in forensic psychology by ABPP, but also members of the American Psychology-Law Society/Division 41 of the American Psychological Association. They obtained 152 responses to a Web-based survey regarding the psychologists' use of a variety of instruments. This study did not focus on specific forensic issues (such as CR evaluations), but on the use of tests in adult forensic evaluations in general. They found that the MMPI-2 and the PAI were the most commonly cited multiscale inventories (followed by the MCMI-III), and the WAIS-III was the most commonly cited intelligence test. Among specialized tools related to malingering, the Structured Interview of Reported Symptoms (SIRS; Rogers, Bagby, & Dickens, 1992) and the Test of Memory Malingering (TOMM; Tombaugh, 1996) were the most frequently cited, followed by the Validity Indicator Profile (VIP; Frederick, 1997).

The results of these more recent surveys are similar to the results reported by Borum and Grisso in 1995. One interesting difference is the rate of acceptance and use of the PAI. This likely is attributable to that test being newer than the MMPI-2; most of the respondents in the earlier study were likely trained prior to the development of the PAI (the average age in that study was 50 years, with 17 years of forensic experience). Furthermore, only recently has the literature been more focused on the application of the PAI to forensic settings (Morey, Warner, & Hopwood, 2007).

Forensic Assessment Instruments

In addition to clinical psychological tests used in forensic practice, there has been increasing interest in the use of instruments designed specifically to assess the legally relevant characteristics of defendants, referred to by Grisso (2003) as "forensic assessment instruments" (FAIs). The three surveys just discussed also included questions about FAIs in regard to CR evaluations. In the Borum and Grisso study, 46% of psychologists reported never using FAIs in CR evaluations, and another 20% reported rarely using them. Archer and colleagues (2006) found similar results 11 years later. The only FAI mentioned by respondents in any of these studies was the Rogers Criminal Responsibility Assessment Scales (RCRAS; Rogers, 1984).

In the Borum and Grisso survey, 66% reported never using the RCRAS for CR evaluations, but Lally (2003) found that 94% of the forensic diplomates in his survey rated the RCRAS as "acceptable" for CR evaluations. Thus, experienced forensic evaluators recognize use of this instrument as acceptable practice, but do not report using it frequently.

It is important to describe the RCRAS in some detail, since it was the only FAI accepted by forensic examiners for use in CR evaluations. (For a comprehensive review, see Grisso, 2003.) This instrument was "designed to quantify essential psychological and situational variables at the time of the crime and to implement criterion-based decision models for criminal responsibility" (Rogers, 1984, p. 1). It thus represents an attempt to provide a more empirical approach to these evaluations, based on quantification of the clinical impairments and specific criteria to guide the evaluator to offer an opinion on the issue of legal insanity.

The instrument, completed by the examiner, comprises 30 data variables, identified in the manual as "Psychological and Situational Variables." These variables are rated by the evaluator on a 5- or 6-point scale (depending on the item), with a 0 indicating no information is available, a 1 indicating no symptoms or disorganization, and 2–6 indicating presence of the factor with increasing degrees of severity. The first 25 items can then be combined into five summary scales with the additional items relevant only to Guilty but Mentally Ill and the M'Naghten standard. The five scales and their components are shown in Table 3.3.

The variables in the RCRAS require clinical judgment in performing the rating, but no objective scoring criteria are presented. The RCRAS then provides a decision-tree model for the American Law Institute (ALI) standard as well as the M'Naghten standard (there is also a model for Guilty but Mentally Ill). The model for both insanity standards first requires a judgment on three variables:

Table 3.3	Rogers Criminal Responsibility Assessment Scales (RCRAS) Variables

A. Patient's Reliability

  1. Reliability of self-report under voluntary control

  2. Involuntary interference with self-report

B. Organicity

  3. Level of intoxication at the time of the alleged crime

  4. Evidence of brain damage or disease

  5. Relationship of brain damage to the commission of the alleged crime

  6. Mental retardation

  7. Relationship of mental retardation to the commission of the alleged crime

C. Psychopathology (at the time of the alleged crime)

  8. Observable bizarre behavior

  9. General level of anxiety

  10. Amnesia for the alleged crime

  11. Delusions

  12. Hallucinations

  13. Depressed mood

  14. Elevated or expansive mood

  15. Level of verbal coherence

  16. Intensity and appropriateness of affect

  17. Evidence of formal thought disorder

D. Cognitive Control

18. Planning and preparation for the alleged crime

19. Awareness of the criminality of the act

20. Focus of the crime

21. Level of activity

E. Behavioral Control

22. Responsible social behavior during week prior to alleged crime

23. Patient's reported self-control over alleged criminal behavior

24. Examiner's assessment of patient's self-control over alleged criminal behavior

25. Was loss of control a result of psychosis?

The items relevant to Guilty but Mentally Ill are:

26. Impaired judgment on the basis of a mental disorder during the period of the alleged crime

27. Psychopathologically based impairment of behavior during the period of the alleged crime

28. Impaired reality testing at the time of the alleged crime

29. Capacity for self-care at the time of the alleged crime

The item relevant to the M'Naghten standard is:

30. Awareness of the wrongfulness of the alleged criminal behavior (includes *moral* as well as legal wrongfulness)

malingering, presence of an organic disorder, and presence of a major psychiatric disorder. If the defendant is deemed not to be malingering but to have either an organic or psychiatric disorder, then the examiner is directed to consider additional factors, dependent on the legal standard. For M'Naghten jurisdictions, the factors are loss of cognitive capacity and relationship of this loss to either the organic or psychiatric disorder. If these factors are considered present, the defendant is deemed to meet the M'Naghten standard for insanity. For ALI jurisdictions, the additional factors are loss of cognitive control, loss of behavioral control, and relationship of loss of control on either of these factors to a mental defect or major psychiatric disorder. If these are present, the defendant is deemed to meet the ALI standard for insanity.

Regarding the RCRAS' psychometric properties, Rogers and Shuman (2000) reported that, in a sample of 76 defendants in an inpatient forensic setting, rater agreements for the diagnostic variables ranged from 85% for malingering ($\kappa = 0.48$), to 88% ($\kappa = 0.79$) for a major mental disorder, to 100% for organic disorder ($\kappa = 1.0$). For the ratings of the components of the insanity defense, the rate of agreement was 87% ($\kappa = 0.75$) for loss of cognitive control and 89% ($\kappa = 0.80$) for loss of behavioral control. The rate of agreement on the ultimate issue of whether the defendant met the ALI standard was 97% ($\kappa = 0.94$). The reliability agreements for individual items was lower, averaging an r of 0.58.

Borum (2003) reviewed the RCRAS and noted that the data on construct validation demonstrated good internal validity. However, it is difficult to assess the external validity of the RCRAS (or any other measure of insanity) due to the lack of a clearly identified comparison measure. For example, Rogers (1984) reported on one study comparing the decision on insanity derived from the RCRAS with the decision made by the court. To avoid contamination, the court was not advised of the RCRAS outcome. In this study of 112 cases, the rate of agreement between RCRAS and legal outcome was 88% (95% for those evaluated as sane, and 73% for those evaluated as insane). The false-negative rate (i.e., those deemed sane by the RCRAS but adjudicated as insane) was quite low, at 4.8%, but the false-positive rate (those deemed insane by the RCRAS but adjudicated as guilty) was significantly higher, at 26.7%. Furthermore, the rate of agreement was highest in cases with either very low or very high

BEWARE
The external validity of any measure of insanity, including the RCRAS, has not been established.

symptom severity, but declined at more moderate levels of symptom severity. This tells us that the RCRAS was successful in identifying cases that courts would consider to qualify, or not qualify, for an insanity acquittal, but it does not necessarily mean that the RCRAS measures the mental conditions that its items seek to identify.

In reviewing the RCRAS, Melton and colleagues (2007) expressed concern that the RCRAS does not meet its intended effect of providing quantifiable measures. The instrument is not able to provide specific, quantitative guidance in how examiners can rate a number of the variables (e.g., relationship between mental retardation and the commission of the alleged crime). This is particularly notable on the summary scales (e.g., loss of cognitive controls), as the rating is not arrived at by adding up scores on the individual items, but rather the examiner is required to use clinical judgment to choose how to weight the individual components. In addition, the RCRAS results in an ultimate decision on insanity, not allowing for a more nuanced or qualified conclusion.

Thus, the RCRAS does not achieve its desired aim of serving as a quantitative measure to assist decisions about criminal responsibility. However, it can be used as "an organizing model or template" (Rogers & Shuman, 2000, p. 238). Utilizing this approach, the RCRAS would be an aid to guide an evaluator regarding which issues to address and a framework for integrating the data into an analysis relevant to the legal criteria.

Studies on Reliability of Criminal Responsibility Opinions

Only a small number of studies have examined the reliability (inter-rater agreement) of evaluator's opinions regarding insanity evaluations. As noted, Rogers (1984) has reported good reliability for evaluators using the RCRAS instrument, which is essentially a structured assessment instrument. Stock and Poythress (1979) reported a very high inter-rater agreement rate, 97%, in a sample of 33 defendants who were *simultaneously* interviewed by pairs of forensic psychologists at a state forensic facility in Michigan, using the ALI standard. The psychologists in the study offered their opinions without conferring with each other. Fukunaga, Pasewark, Hawkins, and Gudeman (1981), in a study of 335 defendants in Hawaii who were evaluated by a pair of psychiatrists, also using the ALI standard, reported a 92% rate of agreement. However, the psychiatrists were able to confer with each other prior to offering the opinion.

Raifman (1979) reported a lower rate of agreement, 64%, in a study of 214 defendants in Arizona, using the M'Naghten test. In that study, each defendant was interviewed by a pair of psychiatrists, one chosen by the defense and one by the prosecution. Phillips, Wolf, and Coons (1998) reported on 66 cases in Alaska (using the ALI standard) in which two or more evaluators assessed the same defendant. They found a rate of agreement of only 76%, despite the fact that the opinions were not necessarily independent of one another.

Three of these four studies are over 20 years old and are not comparable to each other because of differences of methodology (independence of the examiners), legal standard (ALI vs. M'Naghten), and settings (hospital vs. community). Furthermore, as with the research on quality of reports, most of the studies likely reflect on systemic issues and lack of training. The data on the RCRAS are the most positive, in that they suggest that with appropriate structure, reliability can be achieved.

State of Research on Criminal Responsibility Evaluations

As this review shows, the practice of CR evaluations does not have as much empirical support as would be desirable. The problem is not that research challenges the value of CR evaluations, but that too little research has been done. This circumstance is in contrast to the rich body of research that underlies forensic clinicians' evaluations for competence to stand trial (see the other volumes in this series: Zapf & Roesch, 2009; Kruh & Grisso, 2009).

INFO

Research regarding criminal responsibility is limited compared to research on competence to stand trial.

Perhaps the reason for this is in the nature of the objectives of CR evaluations. Competence to stand trial asks questions about the defendant's present mental state. In contrast, CR evaluations require identifying the mental state of a person at some time in the (sometimes) distant past. How to study whether a clinician's judgment about that past mental state is accurate is a conundrum, because no criterion exists with which to judge the clinician's accuracy—that is, there is no independent way to identify the defendant's actual mental state at the past time in question. As a consequence, the research literature does not even tell us whether clinicians' opinions about defendants' psychiatric diagnoses at the time of their alleged offenses are accurate reflections of what their psychiatric conditions actually were at that time (e.g., Poythress, 2004).

Another reason for limited research in this area is the amorphous quality of the concepts associated with the legal criteria for insanity. The standard for competence to stand trial can be translated into several specific abilities (e.g., understanding of courtroom participants and procedures), which in turn can be measured by constructing items that assess those abilities. In contrast, CR inquiries ask, for example, whether certain mental states did not allow defendants to fully appreciate what they were doing or to control their behavior. No one has yet identified a way to validate such an assessment against an objectively measurable criterion. Indeed, as discussed in Chapters 1 and 2, a mental status or behavioral manifestation may be considered exculpable in one jurisdiction but not another.

As a consequence, forensic clinicians do not have the empirical guidance that would be most desirable for conducting CR evaluations. They must rely substantially on clinical knowledge, theoretical paradigms, and adherence to standards of practice in order to obtain relevant data. These data can then be applied in a systematic manner, consistent with the specific legal standard, but the ultimate validity of the conclusions cannot be verified. This has implications that will be discussed in later chapters, regarding the limits of clinicians' CR evaluations and the importance of respecting those limits.

APPLICATION

Preparation for the Evaluation

4

Several ethical and practical issues arise early in the evaluation process, and careful attention to them will avoid difficulties later in the evaluation. Chief among these issues are determining whether the conditions are right to accept the evaluation referral, beginning to search for collateral data, and informing the defendant about the evaluation.

Taking the Referral

Competence of the Evaluator

When a referral is made for a criminal responsibility (CR) evaluation, the forensic clinician must decide whether he has the requisite knowledge, skills, and competence to become involved in the case. This requires a self-assessment. Does the evaluator have the requisite forensic and clinical expertise for the case at hand? Studies that have identified problems with quality of forensic reports (not limited to the area of CR) have suggested that lack of adequate forensic training is a significant factor affecting the quality of the work (e.g., Skeem & Golding, 1998; Packer, 2008).

Prior to accepting a referral, the forensic evaluator should have had previous experience or training in applying her clinical expertise to criminal responsibility cases, as well as relevant experience with populations similar to the individual being evaluated (e.g., Heilbrun, Marczyk, DeMatteo, & Mack-Allen, 2007).

BEWARE
Before taking a referral, be sure you have the relevant knowledge and experience required to act as a CR evaluator for that particular case.

Defendants in criminal cases present with a wide range of disorders, and it is not reasonable to expect evaluators to have extensive experience with each of these disorders. However, the evaluator should have received appropriate training or supervision in performing CR evaluations. Furthermore, if the evaluator does not have experience with the particular diagnostic category, she should be able to obtain and use relevant consultation. For example, a psychologist may need to consult with a medical colleague if the defendant presents with medical illnesses that could impact mental status (e.g., hypoglycemia, hyperthyroidism, etc.). Likewise, psychologists and psychiatrists may need to consult with a clinical neuropsychologist if the defendant has a history of brain trauma or disease that requires neuropsychological testing.

Role of the Evaluator

REFERRAL ISSUE

The evaluator also needs to establish, at the outset, what the specific referral issue is and what role he is being asked to assume. Courts and attorneys may have a variety of questions about a criminal defendant, including issues of competence to stand trial, CR, and treatment or sentencing recommendations. It is important to understand which of these evaluations is being requested, including whether more than one issue is being raised (as is often the case with competence to stand trial and CR). In some jurisdictions, a CR evaluation also requires an opinion about need for treatment (e.g., commitment to a psychiatric hospital), whereas other jurisdictions explicitly bar this issue from being addressed.

BEST PRACTICE

When taking a referral

- Clarify the referral issue
- Beware of attorney bias
- Clarify conflicting obligations

ATTORNEY BIAS

The evaluator's ability to enter the evaluation process impartially may be influenced by the referral source. Zusman and Simon (1983) coined the term "forensic identification" to describe how the clinician becomes identified with the perspective of the retaining attorney. Although they raised this issue in regard to civil cases, the principle applies equally well to criminal cases. The evaluator's objectivity may be compromised by the initial interaction with the attorney. For instance, a defense attorney may communicate as follows: "I have a client with a long history of treatment for schizophrenia who assaulted his brother. The family reported that he was not taking his medications and was acting very bizarrely. We will be pursuing an insanity defense, and I'd like to retain you to be my expert." This introduction may not include other relevant information, such as that the defendant was intoxicated at the time or that he and his brother were arguing over his failure to pay his rent on time. The attorney may or may not purposefully be trying to draw in the evaluator by presenting the client in a manner favorable to the defense. But evaluators should be sensitive to this possibility and remain consciously aware of how the attorney's statements may be biased. The evaluator should delay discussing her opinion with the attorney until a thorough evaluation has been conducted (Rogers & Shuman, 2000). This minimizes the opportunities for the attorney to bias the data-gathering process and the evaluator's opinion.

CONFLICTING OBLIGATIONS

It is also important for the forensic clinician to clarify potentially conflicting obligations, especially dual-role relationships. Guidelines applicable to this issue have been developed by the American Academy of Psychiatry and the Law for psychiatrists (American Academy of Psychiatry and the Law, 2005, for forensic psychiatry in general; and Giorgi-Guarnieri et al., 2002, specific to insanity-defense evaluations) and by the American Psychology-Law Society and the American Academy of Forensic Psychology for psychologists (Committee on Ethical Guidelines for Forensic Psychologists, 1991). For instance, a clear consensus exists among these groups that, except in extraordinary circumstances, a clinician who has served in the past as therapist for the defendant should avoid accepting appointment as a forensic evaluator of that person. This principle has also been articulately explained in the literature (Greenberg & Shuman, 1997; Strasburger, Gutheil, & Brodsky, 1997). Nevertheless, all of the guidelines, while acknowledging the need to be cognizant of dual-role relationships and to minimize their negative impact, recognize that some situations are unavoidable. The psychology guidelines specifically state: "Forensic psychologists recognize potential conflicts of interest in dual relationship with parties to a legal proceeding, and they seek to minimize their effects" (Committee on Ethical Guidelines for Forensic Psychologists, 1991, IV.D.). Similarly, the psychiatry guidelines note: "Forensic Psychiatrists also should be mindful of having multiple roles with conflicting obligations in the same case that may affect their objectivity"(Giorgi-Guarnieri et al., 2002).

Another issue of role clarification arises when forensic clinicians are asked to function in more than one capacity in the same case. The two roles that are most likely to arise in this context are those of the *evaluator* and the *consultant*. The role of evaluator requires an objective, impartial evaluation of the defendant's mental state at the time of the alleged offense. The role of consultant provides more flexibility in terms of the expert's role in providing advice to the attorney about various aspects of the case (including such issues as jury selection and defense strategy). The forensic evaluator begins the process as an impartial participant; the consultant typically is identified as working for the attorney. Mixing the two roles may result in credibility issues for the expert witness (as discussed in Chapter 7), whose objectivity and impartiality may be questioned by the cross-examining attorney. Nevertheless, in some situations, such as court-appointed forensic evaluators for indigent defendants (*Ake v. Oklahoma*, 1985), the practical necessities (i.e., the court will only allocate funds for one expert for the defense to serve both roles) require combining the roles. Although this situation is not ideal, the clinician should nonetheless conduct the evaluation in an objective, impartial manner; once the opinion is formed, the clinician may work with the attorney as a consultant. The significant variable is the evaluator's initial orientation to the case; in order to competently and credibly perform a criminal responsibility evaluation, it is essential for the evaluator to enter the case with an attitude of impartiality, regardless of which side retained his services.

BEWARE
Decline referrals to conduct a CR evaluation if accepting the case would result in conflicting roles (such as therapeutic and evaluative), unless no other viable alternatives exist.

Authorization for the Evaluation

The evaluator should receive explicit authorization from the court or retaining attorney to conduct the CR evaluation. Clear expectations should also be stated about the scope of the evaluation: for example, whether it will address issues of insanity, diminished capacity, need for treatment, or some combination of these. Evaluators should not exceed the bounds of the referral by exploring issues that have not been requested. Furthermore, as noted in Chapter 1, differences exist across jurisdictions in terms of discovery and dissemination of forensic reports. It is essential for the evaluator to clarify at the very outset of accepting the referral to whom the report will be released and/or made available (i.e., whether it will be given only to the defense attorney, to both defense and prosecution, to the court, or to all parties). This will also impact the specific information that the evaluator must provide to the defendant, concerning the limits of confidentiality and privilege inherent in the interview (as discussed later in this chapter).

Timeframe for the Criminal Responsibility Evaluation

Some jurisdictions impose by law or court order a specific timeframe for completion of the CR evaluation. Forensic evaluators should be aware of the specific requirements in the jurisdictions in which they practice, as well as the extent to which flexibility will be afforded. Most significantly, evaluators should not feel obligated to arrive at conclusions to meet a required deadline when the data they have obtained are insufficient for the purpose. In those cases, evaluators should communicate with the court or retaining attorney, explain the circumstances, and request an extension of the deadline. If such a request is not granted, the evaluator will then have to qualify the opinions, explaining that they are limited by the unavailability of certain important types of information. This will be discussed further in Chapter 7 on report writing.

BEST PRACTICE

Be familiar with practices of the relevant jurisdiction regarding the dissemination of your report information and the timeframe for the evaluation.

Seeking Collateral Sources of Information

The central part of any CR evaluation is the evaluator's interview of the defendant. But relying only on the defendant's report is inadequate. Criminal responsibility evaluations require the use of multiple sources of data in addition to interviews with the defendant. Collateral sources, also referred to in the literature as "third party information" (e.g., Heilbrun, Warren, & Picarello, 2003; Otto, Slobogin, & Greenberg 2007) include relevant formal documents as well as information obtained through the evaluator's interviews of people other than the defendant.

Typically, the examiner must have some background on the defendant before interviewing him in order to formulate relevant questions and to have a basis for assessing the meaning of the defendant's answers. As will be discussed in Chapter 5, the evaluation often involves an ongoing "bootstrapping" process of comparing and analyzing data from the defendant and from other sources. However, it is very helpful to have reviewed information about the specifics of the alleged offense prior to obtaining an account directly from the defendant. This allows the evaluator to form an initial impression of the extent to which the defendant's version and the police account are consistent or contradictory, thus providing guidance about further lines of inquiry. Documents related to the alleged offense often include police reports, victim and witness statements, any statements given by the defendant to the police, and grand jury minutes when available. However, the evaluator should not assume that these documents represent the "truth" about the alleged offense; rather, they should be considered as providing data relevant to the evaluation.

BEWARE
Do not simply rely on the defendant's self-report, but corroborate data through third party information. At the same time, do not assume that official documents (such as police reports) or collateral informants provide a full and accurate account.

Collateral Information About the Defendant's History

Collateral information about the defendant's history and background are an integral part of developing a clinical formulation. Documented records, as well as interviews with family members, friends, neighbors, or co-workers, may provide useful information about the defendant's functioning over relevant time periods and at the time of the alleged offense.

DOCUMENTED RECORDS

Relevant documents include official records (such as the criminal record, or "rap sheet"), as well as records of prior inpatient or outpatient treatment (including treatment services obtained during prior periods of incarceration). If the defendant's attorney is requesting the evaluation, she may arrange to obtain the records that the evaluator requests. In court-ordered evaluations, access to records will vary by jurisdiction. In some states, court-ordered evaluations specifically permit release of records to the evaluator without authorization by the defendant. In other jurisdictions, release of prior treatment records requires a release from the defendant, as these are otherwise privileged and confidential documents. In such cases, if the defendant refuses to sign a release, the evaluator should notify the court or the retaining attorney. In some instances, the court may authorize release of the records without the defendant's consent or may limit the defendant's ability to provide evidence relevant to an insanity defense if the records are not made available to the evaluator.

COLLATERAL SOURCES

Unlike medical and mental health records, the defendant's consent is not typically required for the evaluator to contact individuals with whom the defendant did not have a privileged relationship. However, limitations may be placed on the types of information that the evaluator can provide *to* the collateral sources, such as family members, victims, or witnesses. For instance, if the defendant is being evaluated in an inpatient setting where he is also obtaining treatment, the evaluator is not authorized, without the defendant's consent, to share information about the defendant's treatment or mental status.

When contacting an individual who will provide collateral information, evaluators should clearly explain the nature of their

BEWARE
Do not tell individuals that the information they provide will be taken "off the record," as the sources of all data must be included in the report.

role (i.e., providing a forensic evaluation to the court or attorney), the purpose of the evaluation, how the information may be used (i.e., it may be included in a written report and/or in oral testimony, including attribution of the source of the material), and that the individual is not compelled to answer questions, but would be doing so voluntarily (Heilbrun et al., 2003). Some individuals will offer to provide information "off the record"—that is, only if their names are not used and the information is not attributed to them. This request may be genuinely motivated out of a desire not to be perceived by the defendant as providing damaging information or out of concern that they may be called to court to testify at the trial. Evaluators, however, can use only information from an identifiable source. Evaluators are required to acknowledge all their sources of information and to attribute their data to specific sources, in order to provide full disclosure. Failure to do so would be a violation of professional standards for both psychologists (Committee on Ethical Guidelines for Forensic Psychologists, 1991) and psychiatrists (American Academy of Psychiatry and the Law, 2005). Collecting information "off the record" creates an ethical dilemma because the data could influence the evaluator's decision, but would not be transparent, thus not allowing the attorneys and triers of fact an opportunity to evaluate the validity of the evaluator's opinions.

Collateral Information About Facts Surrounding the Alleged Offense

It is often necessary to obtain more detailed information than is available in the official records (such as the police report) about the defendant's behavior, demeanor, and mental state at or near the time of the alleged offense. The best sources of this information are often witnesses and police officers. Evaluators should obtain access to these individuals through the court or attorneys. Police officers (as well as other witnesses) may be reluctant to answer questions from an evaluator calling them unless they have obtained prior authorization from the district attorney. Furthermore, an evaluator can be retained by a defense attorney who does not want to disclose prematurely to the prosecution that an evaluation has been conducted. If the evaluator contacts police or witnesses, this may result in the prosecution learning of the evaluation (for a more detailed discussion of this issue,

BEST PRACTICE
Consult the court or retaining attorney on the appropriate way to obtain access to victims or witnesses relevant to the case.

see Otto et al., 2007). Thus, in such circumstances, the evaluator should inform the defense attorney about the need for such information and agree on a process for obtaining the data.

Special care should also be taken when contacting victims. Particularly, victims of violent crimes and sex offenses should be approached sensitively. In such cases, it is best to have those victims contacted by someone from the district attorney's office (ideally, from a victim/witness assistance unit, if one is available) to inform them that an evaluator would like to speak to them and to determine whether they are willing to be interviewed. The following example illustrates the pitfalls of evaluators calling victims directly. A male defendant was charged with open and gross lewdness for allegedly exposing himself in front of female bystanders in a train station. The evaluator, an eager trainee, found a phone number in the police report for one of the victims and telephoned her. After introducing himself, he discovered the young woman was 11 years old. The evaluator immediately terminated the conversation, concerned about the propriety of asking this young girl to describe the incident in detail. In general, it is important for the evaluator to keep in mind that a victim of violence may be traumatized by receiving a telephone call from a stranger asking for information about her experience. Thus, forensic clinicians should learn from the court or retaining attorney the process by which access to witnesses will be provided.

Initiating the Interview With the Defendant

A key aspect of the interview of defendants in CR cases is assuring that their rights are protected as required by the Constitution and state laws. This requires special attention to informing defendants of the purpose of the evaluation, the evaluator's role, and how information obtained will be used.

Informing the Defendant

For all forensic evaluations, the forensic clinician must begin the interaction with the examinee by explaining the purpose of the evaluation, the clinician's role, and the limits of confidentiality and privilege that will govern the information obtained. This is essential from an ethical perspective, so that the individual is not misled into thinking that the psychologist or psychiatrist is functioning in the usual therapeutic role that the person might associate with those professions.

POTENTIALLY INCRIMINATING INFORMATION

In CR evaluations, the defendant has significant legal rights that must be protected. Since a CR evaluation requires a thorough discussion and analysis of the details of the alleged offense, the defendant might be providing incriminating information to the evaluator. The details provided by the defendant will often constitute a confession to a crime, at least in the sense that the individual acknowledges committing the acts in question. Most jurisdictions provide some protection for the defendant by not permitting information from the CR evaluation to be used to establish guilt, except as rebuttal to a mental state defense. This means that the prosecutor cannot use statements made by the defendant during the forensic evaluation in the guilt stage of a trial to establish that the act was committed. Nevertheless, in jurisdictions in which the forensic reports are provided to the prosecuting attorney prior to a defendant affirmatively asserting a mental state defense, the consequences can sometimes be damaging to the defendant. The defendant's statement, although inadmissible as evidence, may help the state to find other evidence (often called "fruits of the statement") that could be used to prove the defendant's guilt. Thus, as both ethical and legal implications arise as a result of the CR interview, it is particularly important that the defendant understand the purpose of the evaluation, as well as the limits of confidentiality and privilege, prior to participating in the interview and providing potentially incriminating information.

NOTIFICATION OF RIGHTS

The specific details of the notification of rights provided to the defendant about the use of such information will vary by jurisdiction. For example, as discussed in Chapter 1, variations exist in the procedures for dissemination of CR reports, determined by both the referral source and the laws governing evaluations in the particular jurisdiction. In some states, the report will be sent directly to the prosecutor as well as the defense attorney, and in others the defense attorney can review the report before choosing whether to proceed with the defense and have the report released. Thus, the notification provided to the defendant will need to be tailored to the specific circumstance.

The explanation should be framed in simple language and carefully explained. Although it is good practice to provide a written warning and obtain the defendant's signature, simply doing this does not demonstrate that the defendant understood the limitations. Rather, the warning should also be verbally presented and the defendant should be asked to paraphrase or respond to questions to demonstrate his comprehension. Figure 4.1 contains a sample notification, tailored for a jurisdiction in which the reports will be released to all parties. The sentence in brackets would apply in some jurisdictions in which a report is required even when the defendant refuses to participate. In other jurisdictions, the defendant may be barred from introducing her own expert testimony relevant to an insanity defense if she volitionally refuses to cooperate with the evaluation. Evaluators may want to provide even more detail than is given in this sample. Some evaluators clarify to defendants that if they choose not to answer certain questions, this refusal will be documented and reported. The purpose of such a clarification is not to pressure the defendant to participate. Rather, it is designed to provide the defendant with all the information about the nature of the evaluation.

It is important not only to provide this explanation, but also to assess the defendant's understanding. In some instances, the evaluator will determine that the defendant does not comprehend the nature of the evaluation and/or the limits of confidentiality. (Legally, the more important issue is whether the defendant

4
chapter

Dr. Smith is a psychologist appointed by the court to examine you regarding your mental state at the time of the crime for which you are charged (a "Criminal Responsibility" evaluation).

Dr. Smith will not be providing treatment to you and the usual doctor-patient confidentiality will not apply. This means that anything you tell Dr. Smith, as well as Dr. Smith's observations and opinions, may be shared with the Judge, your lawyer, and the prosecutor in a written report. Dr. Smith may also be called to testify in court.

You are not required to participate in the interview and can refuse to answer questions if you so choose. [However, even if you choose not to participate, Dr. Smith is required to submit a report based on other information obtained.]

Dr. Smith has discussed this explanation with me and I have had the opportunity to ask questions. I understand the explanation provided by Dr. Smith.

_____   _____
Signature   Date

_____   _____
Witness   Date

Figure 4.1   Sample Notification of Limits of Confidentiality and Privilege

understands that the information will not be considered privileged communication—that is, that statements he makes may be introduced as evidence in court.) In a court-ordered evaluation, the forensic evaluator may be authorized to proceed even if the defendant does not understand. But the best practice is to consult with the defense attorney first. If the attorney consents to the evaluation on behalf of the client, this should be documented, and the evaluation can proceed. If the attorney does not consent or is not available, the evaluator should contact the court to request guidance. In circumstances in which the clinician is hired by the prosecutor, the recommended course of action is to inform the prosecutor, who can then obtain explicit authorization to proceed from the judge. This issue is not as significant a concern when the evaluator has been retained by the defense attorney who is requesting the evaluation, although it is advisable to inform the attorney nonetheless.

Some evaluators refer to this disclosure as notification of "*Non-confidentiality*" (e.g., Giorgi-Guarnieri et al., 2002). Evaluators should understand that this term is not accurate. Significant exceptions are made to the usual rules of confidentiality, such that the reports can be disseminated to authorized parties and the evaluator may testify in open court; yet other aspects of confidentiality still apply. The evaluator is not permitted to share the information with other parties not involved in the proceedings. Therefore, it is more accurate to refer to the warning as relating to "*limits* of confidentiality."

Involvement of the Defense Attorney

Some defense attorneys may request to be present during the CR evaluation, even when it is court-ordered. The defense rationale is that they want direct, first-hand access to the data provided to the evaluator. However, evaluators often are concerned that the presence of the attorney may interfere with the clinician's assessment, particularly if the defendant is influenced by the attorney or is looking for cues.

The rules for attorney presence may vary by jurisdiction. The majority of courts have ruled that the defendant does not have a right to an attorney's presence during the CR interview and have left the decision up to the discretion of the trial judge (e.g., *People v. Larsen*, 1977; *Commonwealth v. Baldwin*, 1997). However, in some jurisdictions, courts have ruled that the CR evaluation is a "critical stage" of a trial, and thus a defendant has the right to have an attorney present during the interview (e.g., *Houston v. State*, 1979; *Lee v. County Court of Erie County*, 1971).

If an attorney is present during the CR interview, the evaluator should set ground rules to avoid the attorney's interference with the interview and should position the attorney in such a way that the defendant cannot pick up any visual cues. For instance, the attorney may be placed behind the defendant and instructed not to provide any input during the interview (although

BEST PRACTICE
Be familiar with the rules regarding the presence of the attorney and recording of the evaluation, as these vary by jurisdiction. When observation is required, set ground rules to limit the attorney's influence on the defendant's responses.

the attorney may advise the client before the interview begins, or during breaks).

If the interview is recorded in audio and/or video format, care should be taken regarding the administration of formal psychological testing. Consistent with the American Psychological Association's Code of Conduct (2002), providing a recording of the tests could constitute release of testing materials, which would jeopardize test security. Concerns have also been raised by neuropsychologists that not only observers but even taping itself might have an impact on the results of cognitive tests (e.g., Axelrod et al., 2000; Constantinou, Ashendorf, & McCaffrey, 2005), based on the potential for the observers to influence performance, even through subtle means.

The opposing position is that attorneys have the right to have access to any data that will be used at a legal proceeding in which their client is involved. Thus, the argument is that this legal right supersedes the potential variance that could be introduced by the observation. The issue of how significantly the results will be impacted by observation, and whether taping of tests should be legally permitted, is not yet settled, although evaluators have little choice in jurisdictions in which the court explicitly orders that the session be recorded (Committee on Psychological Tests and Assessment, 2007).

Data Collection

The main principle guiding data collection for criminal responsibility (CR) evaluations is to obtain data that will allow the forensic evaluator to develop a clinical formulation that can be applied to the insanity standards. The primary issue is whether the defendant was suffering from a severe mental disorder that could have impacted reality testing or, depending on the jurisdiction, ability to exercise control over behavior, specifically at the time of the alleged offense.

Before examining the types of data to be collected for a CR evaluation, it is worth noting that this data collection process differs from a standard clinical situation. In the latter, the client comes to the mental health professional seeking help, and a patient–therapist relationship is developed based on trust and on the client's expectation that the professional will be supportive and act in his interests. In CR evaluations, even if the psychologist or psychiatrist has been hired by the defense, the evaluator is not an advocate for the defendant. Furthermore, it is important to keep in mind that the evaluee is a defendant in a criminal case and, as such, is highly motivated to present information in a manner designed to bring about a desired outcome. Thus, the evaluator does not begin with an assumption that the defendant will be completely forthcoming. A similar mindset is necessary with other sources of information as well; for instance, police officers or others who describe the alleged offense may have interests in a particular outcome of the case.

This chapter, therefore, describes the forensic approach and mindset required to conduct CR evaluations and then focuses on specific considerations in obtaining three types of information: (a) *historical information* about the defendant's background that may be relevant for forming an opinion about mental disorder, (b) *current mental status information* that may be related to the defendant's mental state at the time of the alleged offense, and (c) *observations of the defendant's mental state and behavior around and at the time of the alleged offense.* This chapter also discusses the use of structured data collection instruments sometimes used in CR evaluations, as well as a variety of considerations for maximizing the quality of one's data.

The Role of the Forensic Evaluator in Gathering Information

Defendants are sometimes motivated to exaggerate psychopathology, in order to appear mentally ill, and to minimize other data that would suggest rational or instrumental motivations for the alleged offense. In other cases, they may be motivated by the opposite desire and try to minimize any psychopathology for fear of being institutionalized and/or stigmatized. Witnesses may be disposed to exaggerate or minimize a defendant's psychopathology at the time of the offense, depending on their own motivations. Thus, the evaluator should strive to maintain a neutral stance and conceptualize the evaluation process as hypothesis-testing, looking to disconfirm or corroborate alternative explanations. Furthermore, even if hired by one side (the defense or the prosecution), the evaluator's task is to provide an objective assessment, rather than advocate for that party's position.

BEST PRACTICE

Maintain objectivity in the evaluation process, initiating your involvement as a neutral evaluator, rather than as an advocate for the retaining party.

Establishing Rapport in the Context of the Evaluation

In terms of approach to the interview, the forensic evaluator needs to strive to establish some rapport, to encourage evaluees to provide useful information. The evaluator, however, should avoid lulling the defendant into a false sense of comfort that she intends to be helpful. This can occur even after the evaluator has carefully explained the purpose of the evaluation and the nature of the relationship, as the interview progresses and the defendant becomes more comfortable and trusting. Although the evaluator is not required to constantly rehash the initial explanation of her role and purpose, if she senses that such "slippage" is occurring, then the defendant should be reminded of the nature of the relationship.

Confronting the Defendant About Discrepancies

Greenberg and Shuman (1997) and Heilbrun, Grisso, and Goldstein (2008) have described significant differences between forensic evaluations and clinical interviews intended for treatment purposes. The forensic examiner is not an advocate for the defendant's position, does not necessarily trust the veracity of the evaluee's report, and is oriented toward objectivity more than a helping attitude. One of the implications of these differences is that, at times, the evaluator may need to be confrontative with the defendant, pointing out discrepancies in the defendant's account.

These discrepancies include both internal ones, such as conflicting accounts that the defendant has given at various times, and external ones, such as inconsistencies between the defendant's self-report and independent observations. For example, a defendant may report being troubled by voices that are interfering with his ability to concentrate during the interview, but shows no evidence of distractibility. At some point in the interview process, the evaluator may need to confront the defendant about these discrepancies. As discussed in the section "Re-interview of Defendant," it is best to reserve the confrontation for late in the interview process, as it is likely to be difficult to reestablish rapport after such an interaction.

Another implication of the nature of the forensic interview is that the evaluator at times may not be fully forthcoming with the defendant. Thus, for example, when probing for malingering, the evaluator may ask the defendant whether she has ever experienced symptoms known to the evaluator as bogus, in an attempt to "trap" the defendant. Indeed, the most commonly used measures of malingering, such as the Structured Interview of Reported Symptoms (SIRS; Rogers, Bagby, & Dickens, 1992), the Test of Memory Malingering (TOMM; Tombaugh, 1996), and the Validity Indicator Profile (VIP; Frederick, 1997), for example, are effective precisely because the defendant is not aware of the purpose of the instrument. Similarly, during the forensic interview, the evaluator will likely ask questions of the defendant without divulging that he knows the information from other sources. This technique can provide some data about the defendant's credibility and her motivation to present accurately.

Historical Information: Interviews and Collateral Documents

Most of the elements of the history-taking required for CR evaluations discussed in this section are similar to those used in standard clinical assessments. Many of these domains are applicable to a diagnostic and clinical formulation, which are then applied to the specific issues related to CR evaluation. In some areas, a specific focus will be placed on data that are particularly relevant to the timeframe of the alleged offense. In addition, two areas that require special attention in all CR evaluations are historical evidence of patterns of substance use and criminal history (e.g., Giorgi-Guarnieri et al., 2002).

INFO

Information applicable to the CR evaluation may include the following:

- Family and developmental history
- Educational history
- Social history
- Employment history
- Mental health history
- Medical history
- Religious history (in some cases)
- Substance use history
- Criminal history

Family and Developmental History

Information about the defendant's family of origin and early history should be obtained. This will include data about any familial history of mental illness and substance abuse. Additionally, data should be obtained about the defendant's early adjustment, including relationships with parents, other parental figures, and siblings, as well as any history of disruption in family attachments, including history of physical and sexual abuse, or exposure to other traumatic events. These data are typically obtained from records, from the interview of the defendant, and, when available, from interviews with family members. In cases in which the alleged victim is a family member, more direct focus will be needed in this area.

Educational History

Information about school history should be obtained from both the defendant and family informants when available. When deemed relevant, official school records may be requested. Educational history includes academic performance, as well as social and behavioral adjustment. What was the extent of the defendant's formal education (how far did the defendant go in school, what degrees were obtained)? How well did the defendant do, in terms of grades? Was the defendant involved in special education or special placements? If so, what was the nature of such placements? Did the defendant drop out of school? Was the defendant suspended or expelled? If so, what were the circumstances? If a defendant appears to present with cognitive limitations, are these consistent with educational achievements? If not, are there data to explain the decline? These data will be particularly relevant if there is a question of mental retardation affecting CR.

Social History

Inquiry should be made regarding the quantity and quality of the defendant's social and intimate relationships, dating back to childhood. Did the defendant have many friends? Was she a loner? Has the defendant maintained friendships over many years? In addition, the evaluator should obtain information about the defendant's history of intimate relationships. This should include data about the number and duration of relationships. These data are useful in terms of a general diagnostic assessment, but require special focus in cases involving domestic violence. In addition, particularly when the alleged offense involved sexual behavior, a thorough sexual history should be obtained.

Employment History

Employment history relates to information about the defendant's ability to obtain and maintain employment, including the number of different jobs held, the length of employment in positions, and the reason for termination. If a defendant has quit jobs repeatedly, or been fired, the circumstances should be explored. This category should also include military history. If the defendant served in the military, which branch did he serve in? How long did the defendant serve, and what were the circumstances of discharge (honorable, dishonorable, general)? In addition, if the defendant served in combat situations, inquiry should be made about possible exposure to trauma and reactions to the trauma. It is important to include information about employment performance around the time of the alleged offense, as this could provide useful information about evidence (or lack of evidence) regarding psychiatric impairment close in time to the alleged offense.

Mental Health History

Extensive inquiry into the defendant's history of psychiatric difficulties is an essential component of all CR evaluations. Does the defendant have a history of a mental disorder or developmental disability? Did the defendant receive mental health treatment? If so, detailed information about the symptoms, as well as a history of treatment, should be obtained from the defendant, knowledgeable informants, and documented records. If the defendant has received inpatient or outpatient treatment, it is important to obtain data about the defendant's initial presentation, as well as his response to treatment. For instance, records of inpatient treatment should include the defendant's presenting complaints and presentation upon admission, course of treatment, response to treatment, and condition upon discharge. Do the data indicate, for example, a diagnosis of a psychotic disorder that is responsive to treatment, but which recurs when the defendant discontinues treatment? If so, was the defendant actively involved in treatment (including taking prescribed medications) around the time of the alleged offense? As will be discussed shortly, the interaction of psychiatric and substance abuse histories is an essential area to explore.

Medical History

It is not necessary to take a full medical history and, indeed, non-physicians are not qualified to do so. However, it is important to obtain information about any significant medical problems that could have an impact on the defendant's mental status. If the defendant has a history of such conditions (e.g., lead poisoning), it should be explored in more detail. A history of head injury, particularly one involving prolonged loss of consciousness, should be explored. If the defendant did experience such an injury (including strokes and seizures), is there evidence of impairments in cognition, mood, or behavior following the injury? Is there evidence of significant change in functioning following the injury? Is there evidence of such impairment close in time to the alleged offense?

Religious History

This area will not be relevant in all cases, but will be particularly important if the defendant presents with delusions or unusual beliefs of a religious nature. Information about the religious affiliation and commitment of the defendant's family of origin would be relevant in such cases, as well as the defendant's subsequent religious identification. It may be of particular interest to help determine whether the defendant's professed beliefs are consistent with a particular religious group or sect, as opposed to idiosyncratic interpretations that might be more indicative of delusional beliefs.

    (An analogous situation arises when the defendant reports that the alleged criminal behavior was politically motivated. In such cases, specific focus on the defendant's political involvement is warranted. The M'Naghten case itself highlights this point, as the political overtones to M'Naghten's thinking have led some [Moran, 1981] to question the extent to which his attempted assassination of the prime minister was motivated by radical political beliefs rather than delusional thinking.)

Substance Use

The data on criminal defendants clearly indicate that the prevalence of substance abuse among this population is high. Furthermore, the co-morbidity of mental illness and substance abuse among forensic

patients is also elevated. As noted in Chapter 2, the implications for the insanity defense of the defendant's use of substances at the time of the alleged offense are quite significant. Thus, the standard history-taking about substance abuse needs to be augmented. Data should be collected from both the defendant and collateral sources regarding the following matters.

HISTORY OF ALCOHOL AND SUBSTANCE USE

The inquiry should include information about

- age at which the use began,

- the degree of usage,

- treatment associated with substance abuse (including detoxification, as well as both outpatient and inpatient treatment),

- functional impairments associated with such use (such as problems in school, work, relationships, violent and/or criminal behavior),

- history of blackouts associated with substance abuse, and

- history of withdrawal effects.

RELATIONSHIP BETWEEN ALCOHOL/SUBSTANCE ABUSE AND SYMPTOMS OF MENTAL ILLNESS

This should include data regarding episodes of psychosis, depression, mania, paranoia, or other disorders that have occurred in the context of alcohol or substance use.

- Does the defendant have a history of such symptoms, independent of such use?

- Are the symptoms exacerbated by use of alcohol or drugs?

- Are psychotic episodes induced by alcohol/substance use but then continue past the period of intoxication?

INGESTION OF ALCOHOL OR DRUGS AROUND THE TIME OF THE ALLEGED OFFENSE

This inquiry should focus on the extent of the defendant's use of alcohol or drugs around the time of the alleged offense, including

- whether the defendant was intoxicated at the time,

- the last time the defendant used substances prior to the alleged offense, and

- any evidence of withdrawal symptoms in the time period following the incident.

It is also advisable to inquire about substance use between the time of the alleged offense and the time of the evaluation. (This could be helpful, for example, in determining whether the defendant's mental status at the time of the interview may be a function of alcohol/substance use that was not a factor at the time period of the alleged offense.)

If a toxicology screen was performed on a defendant close in time to the alleged offense, these data should be obtained as part of the evaluation. The forensic evaluator should obtain the necessary information about the sensitivity of the tests and the time period for which they may be useful (i.e., for each particular substance tested, how long after ingestion the substance would be detected).

chapter **5**

Criminal History

A criminal history should include both arrests and convictions, in juvenile as well as adult court. It is important to obtain official information (such as a "rap sheet") about the defendant's criminal involvement. If possible, the official records should include not only the criminal record within the jurisdiction, but in other jurisdictions nationwide as well (e.g., the FBI's National Crime Information Center [NCIC]).

Typically, such data provide only the names of the charges and the dispositions. Therefore, the defendant should be queried about the specifics of the criminal history. This does not necessarily require a detailed inquiry of every single arrest, particularly with a defendant with an extensive history. However, it is particularly important to focus on crimes similar to the current alleged offense. For instance,

if a defendant claims to have been responding to command hallucinations to rob a bank, it would be instructive to focus, in the history, on previous robbery charges. Was there any evidence that those occurred during psychotic episodes? Were those incidents more rationally motivated (e.g., occurring in the context of needing money to buy drugs)? These data will not be dispositive, but they aid in formulating and testing hypotheses about the most likely explanation for the defendant's recent behavior.

It is also helpful to understand the extent to which criminal activities were engaged in as part of group activity (e.g., gang affiliation or with peers) or as an individual. If the defendant participated in criminal acts along with others, what was his role? Was the defendant the leader of the group, a peer participant, or a vulnerable, suggestible individual taken advantage of by others?

UNDETECTED CRIMES

Evaluators should also be cognizant that not all criminal activity results in an official record, as many crimes are not detected. Therefore, it is useful to question the defendant and collateral sources about other behaviors, which may be relevant to the alleged offense, but that did not result in an arrest. For instance, does the defendant have a history of aggression toward others and, if so, what are the triggers? This may aid in the determination of whether the defendant's violent behavior at the time of the alleged offense was typical of a response to particular provocations or was a function of an acute mental illness.

EXPERIENCE OF VICTIMIZATION

It is also relevant to consider that individuals who have engaged in violent behaviors may also have been the victims of violence. Thus, it is useful to inquire not only about the extent of violent behavior perpetrated by defendants, but also their own experience of victimization. A similar analysis would apply to incidents of sexual offending and victimization.

Current Mental Status Examination

BEWARE
Keep in mind that the defendant's mental status at the time of the interview may not reflect the mental status at the time of the alleged offense; neverthe-less, it may provide a base-line to compare to data obtained about that earlier time period.

A comprehensive and thorough mental status examination should be performed to assess the defendant's mental condition at the time of the evaluation. The defendant's mental sta-tus may be different from her condition at the time of the alleged offense. Nevertheless, observations of current symptoms often can provide information that will assist in devel-oping hypotheses and eliciting data relevant to the reconstruction of the defendant's mental state at the time of the offense. The mental status examination should include an assessment of at least the ele-ments listed in Table 5.1. As with all clinical interviews, the evalua-tor should be sensitive to racial, ethnic, and cultural factors that could influence the defendant's presentation and the diagnostic assessment (e.g., Gaines, 1995; Hicks, 2004; Levine & Gaw, 1995).

5
chapter

Offense-Related Information

This is perhaps the heart of the CR evaluation process. All other data are intended to assist in reconstructing, if possible, the defen-dant's state at the time of the alleged offense. Information specific to that period of time, therefore, is of paramount importance.

Police and Third Party Reports

As discussed in Chapter 4, collateral information regarding the alleged offense is essential to a CR report. Relevant information typically starts with the police report. This source of information should be augmented by any subsequent police investigations, including witnesses' statements, confessions made by the defendant to police, and grand jury minutes. Further information is often nec-essary, and can be obtained by directly interviewing individuals who have first-hand knowledge of the defendant's behavior and func-tioning in the time period relevant to the alleged offense. These may include police officers, victims, witnesses, family, co-workers, and friends. If a defendant was incarcerated or hospitalized shortly

Table 5.1	Areas of Assessment for a Mental Status Examination

Behavior/Demeanor: Defendant's attitude toward the evaluation (e.g., cooperative, sullen, guarded) and behavioral controls (e.g., calm, pacing, etc.)

Orientation: Defendant's awareness of who he is, where he is, and orientation to time

Attention/Concentration: The defendant's ability to attend to and focus on what is being conveyed

Memory: Both short- and long-term memory, including memory for the time period of the alleged offense

Mood: The defendant's level of depression or elevated mood, including data about neurovegetative signs (sleep, appetite, energy level)

Affect: The defendant's observed emotional state, including appropriateness of the affective state and the range of affect

Thought content: For example, delusions, unusual beliefs

Thought process: For example, looseness of associations, tangential communication, circumstantiality

Perception: For example, hallucinations

Insight: If the defendant has a mental illness, does he recognize the symptoms; if the defendant previously reported or manifested acute symptoms that are now in remission, does the defendant acknowledge previous impairments

Intellectual functioning: Estimated level of intellectual functioning based on the interview and history. (If a screen suggests impairments in cognitive functioning, then formal intelligence testing should be pursued.) Most mental status exams also include, relevant to this category, screening for abstract reasoning and knowledge of appropriate social judgment.

Medications: Is the defendant taking any medications at the time of the interview that could affect (positively or negatively) mental status?

after the alleged offense, information about his functioning in jail or in the hospital is likely to be relevant. These data will supplement the self-report obtained from the defendant and/or raise further questions to pursue. It will also likely be necessary to try to reconcile discrepancies from these different sources.

Family members and friends may be especially helpful in identifying the defendant's mental state related to the alleged offense. Sometimes they will have been present, and because they have known the defendant well across time, they can offer observations that compare the defendant's behavior or emotional state at the time of the alleged offense to the defendant's "usual" behavior and emotions. Even when they were not present, they can often describe the defendant's emotions and behavior during the days or weeks leading up to the alleged offense, which in many cases is highly relevant for the logic of developing a clinical formulation to explain the defendant's mental status and behaviors at the time of the alleged offense.

Defendant's Version of the Alleged Offense

Asking the defendant to reflect on the events surrounding the alleged offense will focus on the defendant's description of her behavior, thoughts, and emotions at that time. In approaching this part of the evaluation, it is important to be aware that the defendant is being asked questions about a state of mind at some point in the past, and, in many cases, that point in the past is several weeks, months, or even years earlier. One must always recognize that defendants may have distorted views of their past behaviors, thoughts, or emotions that can impair accuracy. This includes not only the possibility of purposeful distortions (to create a particular impression on the evaluator), but also distortions simply attributable to the difficulty in accurately recalling one's state of mind at some point in the past. This difficulty could be exacerbated if the defendant is in a very different mental state at the time of the interview compared to the time of the alleged offense.

This occurs not infrequently with defendants who were experiencing acute symptoms of mental illness that remitted with treatment by the time of the evaluation. For example, defendants who were experiencing manic symptoms during the time period of the alleged offense may, at the time of the interview, rationalize their previous behaviors, presenting a more coherent and organized version that does not reflect their level of agitation and accelerated thought and motor processes (e.g., Vitacco & Packer, 2004).

APPROACHES TO INTERVIEWING THE DEFENDANT ABOUT THE ALLEGED OFFENSE

Concerning the format of this part of the evaluation, the evaluator should begin with an open-ended approach, asking the defendant for a free-form narrative. The rationale for this recommendation is that it is best to avoid leading the defendant or providing cues as to what is important to focus on. The defendant should also be asked to provide a context to the narrative; that is, rather than asking the defendant to describe what she did that constituted the charges, the defendant should be asked to begin by explaining her circumstances and functioning in the days or weeks preceding the alleged offense (for instance, living arrangements, issues at work, particular stresses, patterns of eating or sleeping, etc.). Information should also be obtained from the defendant about use of medication and substances (e.g., whether she was taking prescribed medications regularly, whether she was drinking or using drugs during that period).

In addition, it is helpful to obtain contextual information about the defendant's relationship to the victim. For example, if a defendant is accused of assaulting his mother, questions should be asked about how they were getting along. For instance, were there issues that were a "sore point" between them?

After providing this context, the defendant should be asked to provide a narrative account of his behaviors and mental state related to the alleged offense. Although, as noted, the defendant should not be led to certain areas, it is often necessary to ask clarifying questions. Evaluators should tailor the questioning to the particular defendant; an individual who is intellectually limited will likely require more structure to be provided by the evaluator. Once this account has been obtained, the evaluator should then probe for relevant details. The specific questions asked will be guided by the defendant's account (i.e., filling in gaps or trying to reconcile internal inconsistencies), as well as by collateral sources of information (i.e., trying to reconcile or explain discrepancies between various accounts).

In obtaining the defendant's account, evaluators should be prepared to ask very specific, probing questions about the individual's thoughts, feelings, motivations, and behaviors. For instance, if a defendant reports feeling "paranoid" at the time, it is important to inquire more specifically. Lay people often use terms such as this in a manner that is different from the clinical significance of the term. Furthermore, it is important to understand the details of this paranoid thinking. Whom was the defendant afraid of? Were there particular individuals or a class of people who were the focus of the concerns? What, specifically, did the defendant think this person or persons intended (e.g., did the defendant feel that her life was being threatened, or did she feel people were making fun of her appearance)? How long had the defendant maintained these beliefs?

Evaluators also should be prepared to inquire very closely about the details of the acts that constituted the alleged offense. The following is an example of such an inquiry regarding a 40-year-old woman, with a history of schizophrenia, paranoid type, who is accused of killing her mother.

Ms. Doe reported that she saw her mother coming down the stairs and thought that she was a witch who was about to cast a spell on her. She stated that she ran to the kitchen, found a knife, and stabbed her mother, who fell to the ground. While her mother lay on the ground, Ms. Doe came up to her and stabbed her four more times.

BEST PRACTICE

Ask specific, probing questions to obtain details about the defendant's behaviors, thoughts, and emotions related to the alleged offense. Do not be satisfied with general descriptions.

A thorough inquiry would involve asking Ms. Doe additional questions, for instance, what, in particular, cued her that her mother was a witch? What happened after her mother fell to the ground? What was she thinking when she then approached her again and continued stabbing? How much time transpired between the first stab wound and the next? What was her emotional state at each point in time (e.g., fear or anger)? Why did she stop stabbing her mother? What was she thinking when the police arrived? These lines of questioning provide useful information about the defendant's mental state at the time of the incident, which will aid in developing a formulation relevant to the issue of criminal responsibility.

ASKING QUESTIONS REGARDING THE COGNITIVE PRONG

Focal questions regarding the specific legal standards should also be pursued. Regarding the cognitive prong, the defendant should be asked whether or not she thought at the time that the particular behaviors would be considered illegal or wrong. If the defendant reports thinking that the behaviors were legal or justified, the basis for this should be explored. What was the defendant thinking at the time that would have justified the behavior? This area needs to be explored in detail. For instance, in the case above, Ms. Doe might have stated that she believed that she thought that the person she stabbed was not really her mother but a witch inhabiting her body and that she felt that killing the witch was the right thing to do in order to rescue her mother and save herself. In other cases, when a defendant reports realizing at the time that the behavior was wrong, further questions should be asked to elicit the rationale for engaging in the act nonetheless.

It is worth repeating, however, that if the defendant reports "At the time, I knew it was wrong," this does not end the evaluator's inquiry. The mere fact that a defendant makes such a statement during the evaluation does not "prove" that it was true at the time of the alleged offense. As noted earlier, many defendants have confused recollections about the thoughts and feelings they might have been having at the time of the offense. Thus, the evaluator should continue to seek other data that might be consistent or inconsistent with the defendant's assertion.

Many evaluators also ask about the defendant's *current* understanding of wrongfulness, in addition to questions about what the defendant believed *at the time of the alleged offense*. This can be helpful if one remembers that this is only one piece of information; by itself, it does not answer the question, and it does not confirm or disconfirm any hypotheses. For example, if the defendant continues, during the evaluation, to justify the alleged criminal behavior due to a delusional belief, this can be explored in detail, including the quality of the defendant's reasoning and reality testing. Then, the evaluator would attempt to determine from other data points whether the behavior at the time of the alleged offense was consistent with this delusion.

Alternatively, if the defendant reports now realizing that the behavior was wrong but was more impaired at the time of the incident, then additional data would be sought to support or disconfirm this possibility. For example, imagine that a defendant states "I know it sounds crazy and that it's not okay to write checks for that much money, but at the time I thought I was a millionaire." The evaluator would look for data to assess presence or absence of a manic episode at the time. In addition, the evaluator would look for data that would be consistent with an explanation that the defendant's current mental status has improved relative to the previous timeframe, or that the alleged criminal behavior was not typical of the defendant's functioning when psychiatrically stable. Of course, the evaluator would also look for disconfirming data as well.

ASKING QUESTIONS REGARDING THE VOLITIONAL PRONG

In jurisdictions that include a volitional prong, the defendant should be queried regarding the elements of choice, planfulness, and regard for apprehension, as discussed in Chapter 2. The inquiry could include questions such as whether the defendant considered alternative courses of action. If so, why were those alternatives not chosen? If not, did the defendant feel that this was the only course of action possible? How long before committing the act did the defendant think of doing it? During that time, did the defendant take preparatory steps? Did the defendant consider ways to avoid detection and apprehension? In the case example of Ms. Doe, the inquiry would include questions about how long she had thought her mother was a witch. Had she considered alternatives to the stabbing, such as escaping from the house? Did she report feeling so frightened at that point in time, that she felt that the only way to save her life was to kill the "witch"? Had she entertained thoughts of stabbing her mother before that day, but inhibited herself? Did she take any steps to avoid being arrested, such as attempting to escape, hide from the police, or deny her involvement?

"POLICEMAN AT THE ELBOW TEST"

When asking about the defendant's reaction to the police, many examiners employ the "policeman at the elbow test." Often it is phrased, "Would you have [committed the act] if a policeman had been nearby observing you?" The rationale for this question is that it is believed to shed light on whether the individual had the ability to control and delay the behavior. Moreover, if the defendant responds in the negative, it is believed to suggest the defendant's understanding that the behavior would have been considered illegal.

Despite the wide use of this question, it is important to consider it as just one piece of information that should not be given too much weight. First, there is no particular reason to believe that an individual can accurately state in the present what he *might* or *might not* have done at some earlier time. A significant body of literature reflects on the limitations of individuals to accurately explain why they behaved in a certain way (e.g., Nisbett & Wilson, 1977). Second, in assessing individuals who have a mental illness (or had one at the time of the alleged offense), it is likely that they are being asked in their present mental state to figure out how they may have reacted when their mental status was quite different, an even more difficult cognitive task.

BEWARE
Do not put too much weight on a defendant's answers to "policeman at the elbow" types of questions. The answer provided by the defendant in the present does not necessarily reflect her thought process at the time of the alleged offense.

Thus, the defendant's answer to the "policeman at the elbow" question may not be relevant to reconstructing her thinking at the time of the alleged offense. In addition, some crimes involve police officers directly (such as resisting arrest, assault on a police officer). The fact that a defendant is not deterred from acting when a police officer is present, therefore, does not necessarily mean that she was unable to control her behavior, only that she *did not* control it. Thus, although asking about the "policeman at the elbow" may help develop further hypotheses, it should not be given undue weight.

This type of question is more likely to be helpful if it elicits specific statements from the defendant about what she was thinking at the time. For instance, if a defendant reports that she saw a police officer nearby and, at the time, thought that she should not enter the store, which she robbed, until the officer left, this would be relevant information (which, of course, would be evaluated in the context of all the other available data). The difference between this response and the concerns raised earlier is that this is a specific statement by the defendant of the content of her thought processes at the time, as opposed to a hypothetical extrapolation. This principle applies to other questions as well that may be posed to the defendant. More relevant than the defendant's characterization of her motivation is the defendant's description of what she was thinking and feeling.

When the Defendant Does Not or Cannot Provide a Coherent Account

Sometimes defendants do not provide an account of the alleged offense. This can occur either when the defendant claims partial or total amnesia, denies being involved in the act, or is too disorganized to convey meaningful information. This complicates the evaluator's task but does not necessarily prevent the evaluation from going forward. The evaluator should approach this issue from a clinical perspective: Are any psychiatric conditions or psychological processes present that might account for the lack of memory?

CLAIMED AMNESIA

In a situation in which the defendant claims amnesia, a careful timeline should be established, including the last thing the defendant remembers before the alleged offense and the first thing remembered afterward. Could the amnesia be accounted for by an alcoholic blackout? If so, there should be evidence that the defendant was never able to recall the incident (since alcoholic blackouts are a function of registration amnesia, as opposed to retrieval difficulties). Are there any other clinical conditions present that might explain why the defendant would be unable to remember the incident? The existence of such clinical conditions should not be equated with a determination that the defendant's mental state at the time of the offense was so impaired as to meet CR criteria. For instance, an individual who is experiencing an alcoholic blackout may engage in rational, goal-directed behavior at the time but just not remember it afterward.

DENIAL OF THE OFFENSE

When a defendant denies committing the offense, it is particularly difficult to comment on mental status at the time. However, even in such circumstances, other sources of information may shed light on the issue. For instance, collateral data may suggest that the defendant committed the offense in an impaired mental state, but the defendant, at the time of the interview, categorically denies having committed the act (or claims to have no memory for the relevant time period). In these situations, it is also helpful to obtain information from the defendant about his functioning in the time periods before and after the alleged offense, as this may aid in developing relevant hypotheses about the defendant's clinical condition at the time of the alleged offense. Furthermore, if adequate data are available from other sources to address the presence/absence of mental illness at the time of the alleged offense, the evaluator could aid the court by providing the relevant information and analysis (even if a full analysis of the defendant's abilities to appreciate wrongfulness and conform conduct cannot be offered).

INABILITY TO PROVIDE A MEANINGFUL ACCOUNT

Similar issues arise when the defendant is acutely psychotic or thought disordered, or too cognitively limited, to provide a meaningful version of events related to the alleged offense. Although this does limit the evaluator's ability to fully probe and obtain information about the defendant's thoughts and emotions related to the specific alleged offense, the observed impairments may be relevant to the clinical and forensic formulation of the case, particularly if the evaluation is being conducted close in time to the alleged offense. Information from third party informants is likely to be particularly helpful in such cases (e.g., "the police officer reported that the defendant was yelling incoherently, referring to the archangel").

Relatedly, there are differences in practice across jurisdictions when evaluations of CR are conducted simultaneously with evaluations of competence to stand trial. Some evaluators will suspend the CR evaluation if the defendant is deemed Incompetent to Stand Trial (IST), while others will continue with the evaluation. There is no established standard in this area, so both approaches are viable. In determining how to proceed in such cases, the evaluator should consider the specific circumstances of the case. The impairments that lead to a finding of IST may or may not interfere with a CR evaluation. For example, if the defendant is being evaluated shortly after the alleged offense and the competence impairments stem from a fixed delusional belief, it is likely that the CR evaluation can proceed. In such a circumstance, useful and relevant information about the defendant's mental status at the time of the alleged offense may be obtained, particularly if the delusion is directly related to the behaviors in question. In contrast, if a defendant is being evaluated many months after the alleged offense, and is grossly thought disordered, with loose associations, it is less likely that information relevant to the timeframe of the alleged offense would be obtained from the defendant.

> **INFO**
> Practices vary by jurisdiction regarding whether or not to proceed with a CR evaluation when a defendant appears incompetent to stand trial. However, impairments in the competence domain do not necessarily prevent the evaluator from conducting a valid CR examination.

Re-interviewing the Defendant

The CR evaluation can be conceptualized as an iterative process in which various issues are scrutinized using multiple sources of data. The evaluator often needs to reexamine those issues in light of

BEWARE
Reserve a confrontational approach for the latter parts of the interview process, as this may result in the defendant being less trusting or willing to share information with you.

additional information obtained. Thus, following the initial interview of the defendant, the evaluator may obtain additional collateral information, as well as test results. At that point, the evaluator is often in a position of needing to re-interview the defendant, to resolve discrepancies or assess the validity of the information obtained.

It is best not to begin this process in a confrontational manner. In such cases, the evaluator should not assume that the collateral information (including police reports) is accurate and that the defendant is dissembling. Rather, the evaluator should present the discrepancies in a straightforward manner and invite the defendant to respond. However, there may be circumstances in which it is necessary to very bluntly inform defendants that their responses are inconsistent or implausible, in a manner clearly conveying skepticism.

Structured Data Collection Methods

Only one instrument has been developed specifically for use in CR evaluations, the Rogers Criminal Responsibility Assessment Scales (RCRAS). Its values and limits have been discussed in Chapter 3. Beyond that, many CR evaluations include psychological testing for cognitive deficits and psychopathology, and these are the focus of this section.

Appropriate Use

Most psychologists perform psychological testing during the CR evaluation (e.g., Borum & Grisso, 1995; Lally, 2003), as discussed in Chapter 3. The criticisms in the literature about use of psychological testing in both forensic evaluations generally and CR evaluations particularly (e.g., Ziskin & Faust, 1995) have focused on the misuse of such tests, noting that they do not relate directly to the legal issue (such as the insanity defense). These criticisms are warranted when evaluators extrapolate too broadly from the testing to the CR issue. But this does not invalidate the appropriate use of test data (Heilbrun, 1992; Goldstein, Morse, & Shapiro,

2003). As discussed by Heilbrun (1992) and Grisso (2003), standardized psychological tests may assist in measuring psychological constructs that are relevant to the legal issue. They should be considered one source of data that can be used to generate or test hypotheses about the defendant's clinical status, while avoiding the notion that they measure legal insanity.

Selecting Tests

In choosing which tests to administer, the forensic evaluator should consider the specific clinical issues relevant to the particular defendant. Thus, if there are reasons to be concerned about the defendant's intellectual functioning, an appropriate test should be employed (such as the Wechsler Adult Intelligence Scale [WAIS-III]). Evaluators may use screening instruments (such as the Wechsler Abbreviated Scale of Intelligence [WASI]) to determine if issues of cognitive functioning may be implicated. However, such screening instruments should not be used as the basis for determining that a defendant was cognitively impaired in a manner that would impact on the CR issue. In such cases, more thorough testing is indicated.

For assessing psychiatric symptoms, as noted in Chapter 3, the most commonly used tests in CR evaluations are the Minnesota Multiphasic Personality Inventory (MMPI)-2 and the Personality Assessment Instrument (PAI), although other tests are also endorsed by experienced forensic psychologists. Such tests typically reflect the defendant's presentation *at the time* of administration, and thus evaluators must be extremely cautious about extrapolating to the timeframe of the alleged offense. A defendant who was acutely manic or depressed when committing a crime may have stabilized by the time of the evaluation and thus not produce a profile suggestive of psychopathology. By contrast, a defendant may decompensate while sitting in jail awaiting the evaluation and thus produce a profile indicative of acute psychopathology that was not present at the time period of the crime.

With these caveats in mind, though, use of such tests may be very helpful in developing or testing hypotheses about the defendant's diagnosis or clinical formulation. For instance, when there

BEST PRACTICE
Choose a test based on its

- Relevance to an element that impacts on the issue of criminal responsibility

- Reliability and validity (e.g., known error rate, peer reviewed)

- Appropriateness for the population applicable to the defendant

is diagnostic uncertainty and lack of a documented history, a testing profile consistent with schizophrenia, paranoid type, may aid in directing further inquiry regarding the defendant's mental status relevant to insanity. Furthermore, some of the scales measure longstanding personality traits, rather than acute states.

Regarding the use of the Rorschach test, as noted in Chapter 3, about one-third of forensic psychologists surveyed by Borum and Grisso (1996) endorse its use in forensic evaluations, including CR evaluations. Weiner (2007) has argued for the utility of the Rorschach in forensic evaluations and cited evidence of its acceptability by courts. However, in the survey study by Lally (2003) discussed in Chapter 3, the Rorschach was categorized as equivocal to unacceptable for use in CR evaluations, and there have been criticisms of its validity, both in clinical as well as forensic settings (e.g., Grove, Barden, Garb, & Lilienfeld, 2002). It is noteworthy that even those authors who criticize the Rorschach acknowledge that there is evidence for its validity in detecting thought disorder (e.g., Lilienfeld, Wood, & Garb, 2000). Therefore, this test may be helpful in cases in which a defendant appears to present with psychotic thinking around the time of the offense, but is guarded or defensive at the time of the interview, making it difficult to determine if a genuine underlying disorder exists (this is particularly the case with individuals experiencing a "first-break" of schizophrenia). In these types of cases, the Rorschach may be employed as one tool, not to directly address the question of legal insanity, but to provide some relevant data regarding whether the individual may indeed have experienced symptoms of a disorder severe enough to have impaired reality testing.

GUIDELINES FOR CHOOSING PSYCHOLOGICAL TESTS
In choosing other tests to administer (both those currently available, and looking forward to new measures that may be developed), the following guidelines are offered.

- *Relevance.* Is the psychological variable that this instrument measures of relevance for the question of CR? Given that the test will not provide direct information about the defendant's state of mind at the time of the alleged offense, will it help to rule in or rule out a type of impairment that *could* impact a defendant's cognitive or volitional capacities relevant to the insanity standard?

- *Reliability and validity.* Does the test have demonstrated reliability? In terms of validity measures, the test should have a known error rate, have been peer-reviewed, and have achieved general acceptance as a measure of the construct. These criteria have been incorporated in the Supreme Court's standards for acceptance of new techniques and methods (*Daubert v. Merrill Dow*, 1993; *Kumho Tire v. Carmichael*, 1999).

- *Appropriateness for the population.* Has the test been validated on a population applicable to the particular defendant? For instance, a test validated only on male defendants should not be used for a female. Similarly, the test should have demonstrated validity with the racial and ethnic groups relevant to the particular defendant.

RESPONSE STYLE

Another very useful function of psychological testing is to aid in the assessment of the defendant's *response style*. As noted earlier, criminal defendants may be motivated to engage either in positive impression management (attempting to minimize psychopathology because they do not want to be seen as mentally ill) or negative impression management (malingering or exaggerating in order to be found Not Guilty by Reason of Insanity). Both the MMPI-2 and the PAI include a number of scales and measures for assessing response style and are therefore useful in this regard. In addition, several instruments have been developed specifically to

aid in detecting malingering or exaggeration of symptoms. As the validity of clinical interviewing techniques alone for detecting malingering has not been established (e.g., Ogloff, 1990; Melton et al., 2007), employment of instruments specifically designed for this purpose should be considered the standard of practice whenever there is a basis for suspecting overreporting of symptoms.

In cases in which there is a question of malingering of psychiatric symptoms, the most highly used and regarded instrument is the Structured Interview of Reported Symptoms (SIRS; Rogers et al., 1992). This instrument contains eight primary scales designed to assess different malingering strategies (Rare Symptoms, Symptom Combinations, Improbable/Absurd Symptoms, Blatant Symptoms, Subtle Symptoms, Selectivity of Symptoms, Severity of Symptoms, and Reported Versus Obvious Symptoms). It has been validated on forensic and correctional populations (e.g., Rogers, Gillis, & Bagby, 1990; Rogers, Gillis, Dickens, & Bagby, 1991).

As with other measures, the SIRS should *not* be considered the ultimate measure of malingering. Rather, the data from the SIRS should be carefully weighed with other available data in arriving at a conclusion about the likelihood that a defendant's presentation is exaggerated or feigned. Evaluators should also keep in mind that individuals who are genuinely mentally ill may nonetheless exaggerate, and thus evidence of exaggeration should not be used to categorically dismiss valid symptoms. These are particularly difficult cases, which require careful weighing of all the available data in order to assess whether the defendant was genuinely experiencing symptoms at the time of the alleged offense that could have impaired the functions relevant to CR.

Other screening measures for malingering have also been developed. These include the Miller Forensic Assessment of Symptoms Test (M-FAST; Miller, 2001), and the Structured Interview of Malingered Symptomatology (SIMS; Smith & Burger, 1997). The advantage of these instruments is that they are very brief and take little time to complete. However, they are designed only to be screening instruments. Thus, if no malingering is detected, further testing may not be necessary. However, if the defendant's scores suggest malingering, then further assessment is required. If malingering of psychiatric symptoms is suspected, then the SIRS should be administered. If it appears that the defendant may be malingering cognitive symptoms, then instruments designed specifically for that purpose are recommended. Among the most widely used and accepted tools for assessment of cognitive malingering are the Validity Indicator Profile (VIP; Frederick, 1997) and the Test of Memory Malingering (TOMM; Tombaugh, 1996). Again, these instruments provide useful data but are not to be used and interpreted outside the context of a thorough clinical evaluation. Furthermore, psychologists should be aware of the limitations of all of these instruments for particular populations. For instance, the TOMM appears to overestimate malingering in mentally retarded defendants (Hurley & Deal, 2006) and elderly demented patients (Teichner & Wagner, 2004).

PROVIDING FEEDBACK TO THE DEFENDANT

In terms of providing feedback to the defendant about test results, the American Psychological Association's Ethical Principles (9.10) indicate that "psychologists [should] take reasonable steps to ensure that explanations of results are given to the individual or designated representative." However, an exception is made for testing conducted in the context of a forensic evaluation. As no clearly delineated standards exist regarding providing feedback to the defendant, the decision about how much information to provide should be determined on a case-by-case basis by the forensic psychologist. One of the considerations is that providing feedback to the defendant may allow the evaluator to correct for errors in testing. For example, both the MMPI-2 and PAI identify evaluees' responses to critical items. It is often helpful to review some of these items with the defendant to ascertain that he indeed intended to answer as he did. Another consideration is that providing feedback may provide the defendant with an opportunity to be more forthcoming. Thus, if results of testing suggest exaggeration of symptoms, sharing this information may induce the defendant to acknowledge feigning and provide more accurate information. When such feedback is given, the evaluator should consider a nuanced approach; confronting the defendant with an accusation of malingering may provoke more defensiveness in an attempt to "save face" (Melton et al., 2007). An alternative approach is to acknowledge the difficult situation that the defendant is in (undergoing a forensic evaluation that could have negative consequences), inform him that there are inconsistencies in the responses, and provide him with an opportunity to reconsider his answers.

A further advantage of providing feedback to defendants is that their responses may reveal information about their personality and credibility. Some defendants will attempt to come up with plausible-sounding explanations for discrepancies and, in the process, create other inconsistencies. Other defendants may acknowledge that they were underreporting symptoms due to feelings of shame. Thus, providing feedback may be a useful clinical technique.

Admissibility of Data

Most jurisdictions allow experts to rely on data that might be considered hearsay if presented by a lay witness. For example, Rule 703 of the Federal Rules of Evidence (and most states have similar rules) states that:

> The facts or data in the particular case upon which an expert bases an opinion or inference may be those perceived by or made known to the expert at or before the hearing. If of a type reasonably relied upon by experts in the particular field in forming opinions or inferences upon the subject, the facts or data need not be admissible in evidence in order for the opinion or inference to be admitted.

In CR evaluations, such sources of data would include medical records, as well as information from collateral sources. Nevertheless, not all such information will be deemed admissible, as discussed next.

Admissibility of Third Party Information

In the New York case of *People v. Goldstein* (2005), the Appeals Court reversed a conviction in an insanity case, ruling that specific statements made by third parties to the prosecution's psychiatric expert should not have been admitted into evidence, without the defendant being able to cross-examine the parties directly. In arriving at this ruling, the Appeals Court first had to decide whether the information was of the type reasonably relied upon by forensic mental health experts. The Court ruled that such third party information is accepted in the profession. However, the Court then decided that since these statements had probative value, the defendant had a right to confront the witnesses. Since the witnesses were not available at trial, the Court ruled that the psychiatrist should not have been allowed to repeat these statements in her testimony.

Although this ruling was specific to New York, similar issues are likely to arise in other jurisdictions as well. It is noteworthy that Federal Rule of Evidence 703, cited earlier, was modified in 2000 to include the following caveat:

> Facts or data that are otherwise inadmissible shall not be disclosed to the jury by the proponent of the opinion or inference unless the court determines that their probative value in assisting the jury to evaluate the expert's opinion substantially outweighs their prejudicial effect.

This modification reflects the concern that, although this information is relied upon by the expert (for example, in establishing mental status elements), the statements repeated by the expert could be perceived by the jury as establishing factual accuracy.

Forensic clinicians are not expected to possess a sophisticated legal understanding about the rules of hearsay and admissibility of various forms of evidence. However, it is helpful to be aware of potential problems with admissibility, to guide the data collection process. For example, in the *Goldstein* case, the psychiatrist testified that a collateral source informed her that the victim bore a remarkable resemblance to another woman who had previously teased the defendant, thus supplying a possible motive. The Court noted that the psychiatrist could have arrived at the same conclusion

based on other data that had been admitted. This was not a criticism of the psychiatrist, who had no reason, at the time, to think that the information she obtained would be ruled inadmissible. However, it illustrates that when there is a question of whether a particular piece of information is legally admissible, there may be ways of obtaining corroborating data that *will* be admitted into evidence.

Unadjudicated Criminal Behavior

Another type of information that raises issues of admissibility involves a defendant's report of other criminal behavior that has yet to be adjudicated (i.e., open charges distinct from those being evaluated) or previously unreported offenses (i.e., unknown to the police or prosecutor). There are both legal considerations of admissibility as well as professional ethical responsibilities raised by such disclosures. Rogers and Shuman (2000) recommend a highly conservative approach to including such information in the report, unless the evaluator believes that it is "highly probative of the defendant's mental status at the time of this offense" (p. 302). In making such a determination, the evaluator should consider issues such as closeness in time between the current alleged offense and the other offense, as well as similarity of the offenses.

Adequacy of the Data

Evaluators often are faced with a situation in which collateral sources are not accessible or do not return calls. Similarly, records of previous treatment may have been requested but not have arrived by the time the report is due. Evaluators should always document their efforts to obtain specific information that they thought might be relevant but that they were not able to obtain. If the evaluator believes that the missing data are so crucial that an adequate evaluation cannot be completed without them, the court or referring party should be so notified. However, if the data would be helpful but do not preclude the evaluator from arriving at a conclusion, this should be noted and the report completed. As described in Chapter 7, circumstances such as these sometimes require that evaluators offer "qualified" opinions, recognizing that the unavailable information might have impacted their conclusions.

BEST PRACTICE

Note any missing information or conflicting fact patterns in your report and how these impact on the opinions offered.

Other circumstances arise in which the problem is not lack of access to data, but rather conflicting factual data. For instance, significant factual differences may exist in the accounts provided by the defendant and the alleged victim. When these discrepancies do not reflect distortions in reality testing on the defendant's part, but rather plausibly differing accounts, the evaluator will need to make that clear to the court and, if necessary, explain how the forensic opinion might be different depending on which set of facts the trier of fact determines to be more accurate.

5
chapter

Interpretation 6

Having collected the data, the evaluator must interpret it to give it meaning for use in addressing the question of criminal responsibility (CR). In this chapter, the interpretive process to be used by evaluators in CR cases, as well as common errors in analyzing data, are discussed.

The Logical Process of Interpretations in Criminal Responsibility Cases

Almost all treatises on forensic mental health evaluations urge evaluators to use scientific reasoning to assess the causal connection between data and the psycholegal conclusions. Although the forensic evaluation process does not lend itself to formal scientific experimental standards, the logic employed in scientific reasoning can be applied to the data. The interpretation process in CR evaluations is a recursive one; as data accumulate, one or more hypotheses should be generated, and additional data relevant to those hypotheses should be sought out. The evaluator should frame the hypotheses in clinical terms and then apply them to the forensic issue. Table 6.1 gives five examples of hypotheses that could be developed in CR cases.

Considering Contradictory Data and Multiple Explanations

In approaching a case, it is useful to maintain a flexible mindset and allow the data in the individual case to form the basis of the analytic process. Consistent with principles of scientific reasoning, it is essential to consider explanations that would disconfirm the hypothesis

Table 6.1	Examples of Hypotheses for Criminal Responsibility Cases

- The defendant demonstrates symptoms consistent with a mental illness.

- The defendant's mental state at the time of the alleged crime can be attributed to acute intoxication.

- The defendant's reality testing was significantly impaired at the time of the alleged crime.

- The defendant acted in response to delusional beliefs.

- The defendant's behavioral controls were significantly impaired by symptoms of a psychiatric disorder, most likely a manic episode.

developed, rather than focusing only on finding data to support the hypothesis. The latter approach distorts both the data collection process and the data analysis, as it promotes only selective attention to particular data points and ignores contradictory data. For example, if a defendant reports committing the offense in response to command hallucinations, the evaluator should not *only* seek out evidence of other reports of auditory hallucination by the defendant. Rather, the inquiry should also include looking for disconfirming data, such as evidence of discrepancies between the presentation during the forensic interview and behavior on the hospital unit, a "fake-bad" profile on the Minnesota Multiphasic Personality Inventory (MMPI)-2 or Personality Assessment Inventory (PAI), or a profile on the Structured Interview of Reported Symptoms (SIRS) that is indicative of malingering.

In many instances, the data will not be clear, and it will be necessary for the forensic clinician to consider multiple explanations for certain behaviors. Forensic evaluators should endeavor to determine which explanation is the *best* fit for the data, while acknowledging the alternative explanations. This principle is particularly important in CR evaluations, because of the retrospective nature of the evaluation.

As the task is to reconstruct a state of mind at some point in the past, current measures are not directly dispositive of the issue. Therefore, the accumulated weight of the data needs to be assessed.

BEST PRACTICE

Test your hypothesis by considering alternative explanations. In the case of unclear data, determine which explanation best corresponds to the information available.

The most direct information comes from the defendant. This often provides the basis for the initial hypotheses, which are then corroborated or disconfirmed with the additional data sources. An essential issue to address, therefore, is the validity of the defendant's presentation of his clinical status. This is *not* equivalent to determining whether the defendant provided a truthful account. Psychologists and psychiatrists are not "lie-detectors," but can assess the internal and external consistency of the defendant's presentation. The forensic clinician can thus conclude (if adequate data are available) whether the defendant's reported mental state at the time of the alleged offense is consistent with known elements of a clinical disorder and consistent with the actual behavior, as well as external observations. Similarly, the evaluator should be sensitive to indications that the defendant may be underreporting symptoms and attempting to portray himself as acting more rationally at the time of the alleged offense than he really was.

Relationship of Mental State at Time of Interview to Mental State at Time of Offense

The principle interpretive task in CR evaluations is to decide whether the defendant was experiencing symptoms at the time of the alleged offense, and if so, whether they impaired her cognitive and/or volitional capacities at the time of the alleged crime. It is important to consistently and clearly keep in mind that data will be obtained about the mental state of the defendant at two different points in time—at the time of the interview, and at the time of the alleged crime—and that one should not automatically be inferred from the other. The nature of most psychiatric disorders is such that fluctuations occur in the severity of symptoms, and the presentation can also be impacted by stressors, as well as treatment or lack of treatment. Even with more stable disorders, such as mental retardation, the defendant's functioning may be improved with structure (such as in a psychiatric hospital during the evaluation period) or may deteriorate under stress (such as being arrested and incarcerated). Therefore, evaluators must determine the applicability of observed or reported symptoms to the previous timeframe.

The next level of analysis required is to determine the relationship between the clinical symptoms present at the time of the alleged offense and the specific behaviors that constitute the crime. There may be no relationship, an indirect one, or a direct one. This is a significant issue that will have implications for the decision about whether the defendant's abilities relevant to the cognitive and/or volitional prongs were substantially impaired by the disorder.

THE CASE OF NO RELATIONSHIP

The evaluator may find that, despite the presence of some symptoms, these symptoms did not have an impact on the defendant's motivation, thinking, or behavioral control related to the specific alleged offense. For example, a defendant, who reported ongoing delusional beliefs about his neighbors conspiring against him, attacked and stole money from a homeless individual in a train station. He reported that he stole the money because he was hungry and had no money on him. Collateral data from witnesses and the arresting police officers confirmed that the defendant did not make any paranoid statements about the victim, attempted to avoid detection, and denied when arrested that he had stolen the money. Thus, despite clear data about the presence of an encapsulated delusional system, there is no apparent connection between this symptom and the criminal behavior.

THE CASE OF A DIRECT RELATIONSHIP

A direct relationship exists when a defendant's symptoms can be tied directly to the alleged offense. Thus, if the defendant in the previous example attacked his neighbor because he thought this neighbor was assaulting him with harmful microwaves, this would represent a direct relationship between the disorder and the act. Establishing such a direct relationship does not mean per se that the defendant's abilities related to the cognitive and/or volitional prongs were substantially impaired; rather, it provides the basis for further analysis of this issue. In this case, the evaluator would explore the defendant's state of mind at the time, including the level of distress, his perception of alternative courses of action available, whether he felt that he was in imminent danger, and whether anything else about the event is consistent or inconsistent with the defendant's account of his state of mind.

BEST PRACTICE

Determine if a relationship exists between the defendant's symptoms and the alleged offense and, if so, if the symptoms had a direct or indirect impact.

THE CASE OF AN INDIRECT RELATIONSHIP

A defendant may have symptoms that provide motivation for the offense, but do not directly impact on the functional capacities relevant to the insanity defense. An interesting example was provided in the discussion related to the development of the American Law Institute (ALI) insanity defense (American Law Institute, 1985). This hypothetical example involved a defendant who delusionally believed that he would inherit a great deal of money if a relative died. To obtain these funds, he killed this person. This defendant's distorted thinking led him to a mistaken belief about his ability to inherit the money; that is, without the delusion, he would not have developed a reason to kill his relative. However, this symptom did not reduce his ability to appreciate that it was wrong to kill the relative.

6
chapter

Relevance of Symptoms to the Legal Standards

As this discussion demonstrates, the directness of the relationship between symptoms and the criminal act is relevant to the legal standard but is not determinative. Additional analyses are required to tie the symptoms to the specific cognitive and/or volitional prongs in the particular jurisdiction. For the cognitive prong, for example, the focus will often be on the nature of the defendant's reality testing and the relationship between any impairments in this realm and ability to understand or appreciate that the particular behaviors engaged in would be considered illegal or wrong. In this regard, the *content* of the defendant's thinking is relevant, but it is also important to

focus on the *quality* of the thinking. For example, a defendant may endorse a belief system that does not recognize the validity of government laws. However, for the purposes of the insanity defense, it will be essential to distinguish between an individual with extreme political beliefs and one whose beliefs are considered delusional in that they are based on inherently irrational and distorted thinking. In addition to analyzing the data about the defendant's thought processes, the evaluator will also utilize collateral sources of information about the defendant's statements and behaviors around the time of the alleged offense.

Interpretations Involving Substance Abuse

Teasing apart the relative contributions of a mental disorder and the effects of substance abuse, when both elements are present, is one of the more difficult tasks in CR evaluations. For instance, a woman with a history of bipolar disorder is charged with breaking and entering into a house. She reports that she thought she was entering her own home and was surprised to find a "stranger" there. She also acknowledges drinking heavily that day, and the victim reported that the defendant was slurring her speech, appeared intoxicated, insisted that it was her home, and was speaking rapidly in a manner that was difficult to follow. The evaluator is able to conclude, from all the data available, that the defendant's ability to appreciate that it was wrong to enter the house was impaired, as she genuinely believed that she owned the home in question.

The alternative hypotheses to be considered would be: (a) that her confusion and disorientation were due to her bipolar disorder, (b) that these were symptoms of acute intoxication, or (c) that the symptoms were a combination of both. The evaluator would need to consider a number of other pieces of data: What was the defendant's behavior and presentation in the hours and days prior to this incident? Was she taking her prescribed medication? Is there evidence that she was exhibiting manic symptoms prior to drinking that day? How long did her impaired mental status last after the incident? (Did her symptoms subside within hours, once her blood alcohol level declined, or did she continue to manifest manic symptoms for a period of days?)

Based on the answers to these and similar questions, the evaluator would propose a formulation that would best account for the data. The evaluator could conclude that the defendant's impairments were primarily a function of her bipolar disorder and were exacerbated by her drinking. Alternatively, the conclusion could be that the defendant was psychiatrically stable but became impaired only during the acute period of intoxication, after which her mental status stabilized. A third possibility is that the defendant's mental status was stable until she began drinking, at which point she developed a full-blown manic episode that persisted for a period of days or weeks. In some cases, the data will allow a clear determination; in other cases, the evaluator will not be able to distinguish between the hypotheses and will have to explain the limitations of the available data.

See Figure 6.1 for a comprehensive diagram of the interpretive strategy for insanity evaluations.

Common Errors When Interpreting Criminal Responsibility Data

6
chapter

The following types of errors in interpretation come from two sources. Some have been culled from the literature (e.g., Nicholson & Norwood, 2000; Wettstein, 2005; Knoll & Resnick, 2008). Others derive from the author's experience performing quality assurance reviews of forensic reports in several jurisdictions, as well as serving on a panel that reviews practice samples for the American Board of Forensic Psychology. This list is not exhaustive, but it demonstrates some of the most common problems in reasoning found in CR reports.

Illusory Correlation

Conclusions regarding the relevant CR prongs must be based on an explanation of how clinical impairments actually influenced the defendant's behavior. Nevertheless, some evaluators focus

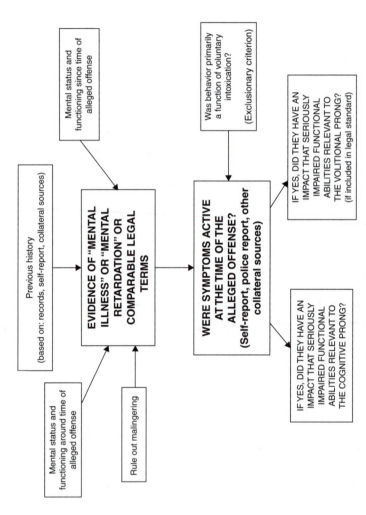

Figure 6.1 Interpretive Strategy for Insanity Evaluations

BEWARE
Common errors found in CR reports include the following:

- Making an "illusory correlation"; that is, presuming that because a defendant was experiencing a mental disorder at the time of the offense, the disorder is the primary cause of the behavior

- Reasoning with uncorroborated information; that is, making an interpretation without validating data through collateral sources

- Failing to consider alternative explanations; that is, not seeking out or considering contradictory data

- Overreaching; that is, arriving at a conclusion that goes too far beyond the data at hand

- Not fully understanding the relevant psycholegal constructs; that is, assuming an interpretation of some of the elements of the insanity defense rather than being guided by statutes or case law

almost entirely on establishing a diagnosis, then conclude that the diagnostic condition impaired ability to appreciate wrongfulness or control behavior. This results in an analysis that is inadequate to explain *how* the disorder caused the impaired ability. The error here is presuming that because the mental illness and the criminal behavior occurred together, the former was the cause of the latter. This type of error is called *illusory correlation*. The mere co-existence of a disorder and a behavior does not mean that the disorder caused the behavior. It is important to keep in mind that there is no one-to-one correspondence between any clinical diagnosis or symptom presentation and the insanity defense.

For example, a woman assaults a co-worker and reports that the victim had been plotting against her. The evaluator then concludes that the assault was a function of the delusional belief. Although this is one plausible hypothesis, the causal connection has not been established. Alternatively, the victim may have made a derogatory comment, which the defendant understood without distortion and reacted to out of anger. Often, careful probing about the details surrounding the alleged offense can help to avoid this type of error by focusing on specifics that are relevant to a causal analysis.

Reasoning With Uncorroborated Information

As discussed in Chapter 4, one of the most important imperatives in forensic evaluations is the need to obtain valid collateral sources of information. In contrast, evaluators sometimes rely exclusively on the clinical interview and a brief police report, without obtaining more detailed information. This results in an interpretation that is based on uncorroborated data—that is, without information to judge its consistency with some other source.

Even when the police report is reviewed, this document is not always sufficient to convey the level of detail required for a CR evaluation. The officer writing the report is likely not to be attuned to the specific symptoms or behaviors that a psychologist or psychiatrist would understand in the context of a mental disorder. Furthermore, witnesses, as well as informants who are familiar with the defendant, may provide information that is not consistent with the defendant's claims. This works in both directions—sometimes the collateral sources could provide data indicating either more or less psychopathology than the defendant reports.

The error of reasoning with uncorroborated information is often seen in ambiguous cases in which the level of the defendant's functioning around the time of the alleged offense is unclear. It also emerges when lack of clarity exists about the relationship between substance abuse and the defendant's mental state. Third party informants may provide very useful information in such cases to help disentangle conflicting or ambiguous data.

Failure to Consider Alternative Explanations

As previously noted, scientific reasoning requires consideration of hypotheses and evaluation of data that either are consistent with the hypotheses or disconfirm them. Evaluators sometimes focus too early on only one explanation and then adduce data consistent with it, without seeking out or considering alternatives. This interpretive error can begin early on, if the evaluator approaches the interview with preconceived notions (as noted in the discussion of forensic identification in Chapter 4). However, even if the evaluator maintains initial impartiality, once an explanation is formulated, the evaluator may narrow the interpretive focus and not consider contradictory data.

This phenomenon, known as the *confirmation bias*, has been studied in various contexts (e.g., Nickerson, 1998). This is a particularly seductive error in legal settings, since it conforms to the adversarial system. In the legal system, each side builds a case consistent with its own views and is not obligated to present alternative explanations. However, forensic mental health professionals should be constrained by the requirement to be objective and test alternative hypotheses. The "antidote" for this type of error is for the evaluator, after arriving at a possible explanation, to consciously and deliberately ask whether data are available (or could be obtained) that would refute that explanation.

Overreaching

Sometimes evaluators obtain an account from the defendant as well as from collateral sources, but then arrive at a conclusion that goes too far beyond the data at hand. This can occur particularly when the data obtained are ambiguous or elements are missing (e.g., a relevant informant is not available, the defendant's memory is too vague, there is a question of intoxication at the time of the alleged crime but no confirmation can be obtained, contradictory accounts are offered by witnesses and cannot be reconciled). This error may result from a tendency to endorse too strongly the "most likely" explanation even if the data are insufficient to support it, or from perceived pressure to provide a conclusive opinion. Lawyers and judges often do prefer that an expert be more definitive, and the forensic evaluator may try to accommodate the "client." However, the appropriate response is to offer a qualified opinion, including an explanation of why a stronger opinion cannot be offered, rather than rely on inadequate data to bolster a conclusion.

Some clinicians overreach in their use of structured instruments like the Rogers Criminal Responsibility Assessment Scales (RCRAS). Although the RCRAS guides the examiner to an ultimate opinion about whether the defendant met the legal standard, the instrument should not be considered equivalent to the legal standard. Thus, a report stating that: "Based on the RCRAS, the defendant meets the M'Naghten criteria for being considered legally insane" is overstating the relationship between the data obtained and the conclusion. Rather, the RCRAS can be used to help guide the data collection and analysis process, but the opinion offered should be based on the totality of the data, and a fuller articulation of the relationship between those data and the conclusions reached.

Lack of Understanding of the Relevant Psycholegal Constructs

As discussed in Chapter 2, no unanimity of legal opinion exists regarding the interpretation of some of the elements of the insanity defense. Thus, for example, jurisdictions differ in interpretation of "wrongfulness." Evaluators sometimes assume a certain interpretation, such as focusing only on the defendant's understanding of the illegality of the behavior (as opposed to moral wrongfulness), without a legal basis for such an interpretation. Similarly, in situations in which a defendant is intoxicated and also manifests symptoms of a mental illness, evaluators who are not sufficiently versed in the relevant concepts may make assumptions about whether the presence of substance use precludes consideration of the insanity defense. This type of error also extends to opinions about what constitutes a mental illness or mental retardation. The standards that would be applicable in a treatment context may not be the same as those used in a legal situation (as determined by statutes or case law).

Report Writing and Testimony | **7**

Relevance, clarity, and completeness are the chief requirements for conveying data and interpretations to attorneys and courts. The written criminal responsibility (CR) report is perhaps the most important mode of communicating the evaluator's data and conclusions, because many cases in which the CR question has been raised do not proceed to trial, when oral testimony would be required. In addition, the written report informs attorneys about the evaluator's conclusions and allows further determination of how the case will proceed. Therefore, it is important that the report be written clearly, with adequate documentation of the sources of data, the relevant data points, and a clear articulation of the relationship between the data and the conclusions offered. Finally, if the written report is prepared carefully, it becomes a guide for the expert testimony.

Writing the Criminal Responsibility Report

When a CR evaluation is court-ordered, a full, comprehensive report is always required. This usually also will be the case when attorneys request the evaluation. However, in some circumstances, it is reasonable either not to prepare a written report or to provide a less-detailed one (Giorgi-Guarnieri et al., 2002; Rogers & Shuman, 2000). This is most likely to occur when the expert is hired by the defense in a jurisdiction in which the report is discoverable by the prosecution (e.g., *Edney v. Smith*, 1976). In such cases, the defense may not want incriminating statements made by the defendant released to the prosecuting attorney when a decision has not yet been finalized regarding the use of the insanity defense. Furthermore, when the forensic evaluator is privately retained by either side, attorneys may reasonably request verbal feedback prior to submission of a written report, with an understanding that, if the evaluator's opinion is not supportive of the attorney's position, then a report will not be produced and the evaluator will not be called to testify. This also avoids having the attorney pay for the expert's time to write a report that will never be used. However, in situations in which the evaluator is to testify, there is no justification for failing to produce a report.

The most significant guiding principle in writing a CR report is that the reader should be able to fully understand the conclusions offered and the bases for those conclusions. Thus, the report should be clearly written, in language comprehensible to the lay reader (i.e., non–mental health professional), and the relationship between the data and conclusions should be explicitly articulated, including attributing all data used to the sources of that information.

Clarity of the Report

As noted in Chapter 3, some evidence suggests that judges and lawyers often do not understand even basic technical terms routinely employed by mental health clinicians. Although Melton and colleagues (2007) and Heilbrun (2001) suggest that forensic evaluators minimize the use of technical terms, another way to construe best practices is to avoid the use of *unexplained* jargon. Technical terms do have the advantage of being more concise and thus contribute to readability of reports, provided that the terms have been defined. Evaluators should routinely define all technical terms the first time they are used, but may use these terms subsequently in context. For example, an evaluator may note in the mental status section of the report that a defendant did not report "auditory hallucinations, i.e., hearing imaginary voices," and subsequently use the term without explanation in the conclusions section. Standardized definitions of psychiatric and psychological terms can be adapted from a number of

BEST PRACTICE

Define technical terms used in the report to make them more intelligible to the lay reader.

sources such as the *Diagnostic and Statistical Manual of Mental Disorders, Fourth Edition, Text Revision (DSM-IV-TR*, APA, 2000), or the *American Psychological Association's Dictionary of Psychology* (VandenBos, 2006).

Model Format for Criminal Responsibility Reports

Almost all guides for writing forensic reports suggest that they be written in sections, as this aids in the creation of a clear and organized report. In addition, by separating the reports into discrete sections, the forensic evaluator can distinguish between *data* and *interpretations*. The data sections should include all the relevant information that bears on the defendant's mental state and the CR issues. Then, interpretations should appear in a conclusion section containing the evaluator's opinions and the specific reasons for those opinions. New data should *not* be introduced in the conclusion section; rather, that section should be reserved for analysis and interpretation of the data. Furthermore, the data sections should be organized in a manner that clarifies the type of information included.

The following is a guideline for CR report sections, based on models proposed in the literature (Rogers & Shuman, 2000; Heilbrun, 2001; Giorgi-Guarnieri et al., 2002; Melton et al., 2007; Knoll & Resnick, 2008). It is important to keep in mind that this is being offered as a guideline, as there is no "correct" model; forensic evaluators can employ different formats, as long as all the relevant information is conveyed in a coherent, comprehensible manner. Appendix B contains a checklist, which may be useful for evaluators to consult to determine if their reports have incorporated all the recommended elements.

IDENTIFYING INFORMATION

Begin by identifying information about the defendant, including the specific charges faced, as well as the referral source (i.e., the defense attorney, the prosecutor, the court), and referral issue (e.g., insanity, diminished capacity, etc.).

BEST PRACTICE

Although there is no one correct model for writing CR reports, use a format that assists in clearly communicating data and interpretations.

Table 7.1 | Suggested Sections and Order for the Criminal Responsibility Report

---

   I. Identifying Information

  II. Sources of Information

 III. Notification of Limits of Confidentiality/Privilege

 IV. Legal Standard

  V. Historical Information

 VI. Mental Status/Clinical Functioning

VII. Results of Psychological and/or Medical Tests

VIII. State's Version of the Alleged Offense

 IX. Other Persons' Descriptions of the Defendant or Alleged Events

  X. Defendant's Version of the Alleged Offense

 XI. Clinical Opinions Relevant to the Issue of Criminal Responsibility

The date of the report, as well as the date of the alleged offense, should also be included.

SOURCES OF INFORMATION

It is essential to document the evaluation methods, listing all sources of information, including

- the clinical interview with the defendant (dates and time spent),
- documents and records reviewed,
- collateral sources contacted, and
- tests administered or reviewed.

If unsuccessful attempts were made to obtain records or contact collaterals (i.e., records were requested but not received, collaterals could not be located, or telephone calls were not returned), these should be noted too. This demonstrates that the evaluator did not overlook relevant sources of information. The careful documentation of sources of information is considered a best practice in most references on forensic report writing (e.g., Heilbrun, 2001). Detailed documentation provides the reader with a greater ability to assess the credibility of the information and the weight to be given to it, particularly, although not exclusively, when conflicting accounts need to be reconciled.

NOTIFICATION OF LIMITS OF CONFIDENTIALITY/PRIVILEGE
The report should contain an explicit description of what the evaluator told the defendant about

- the evaluator's role (i.e., that the evaluator is a psychologist or psychiatrist, performing a forensic evaluation),

- the purpose(s) of the evaluation (e.g., insanity, diminished capacity, competence to stand trial, or a combination of more than one purpose), and

- the limits of confidentiality and privilege (i.e., with whom the information obtained will be shared, including both the written report and any verbal communication, including testimony).

The evaluator should include an assessment of whether the defendant understood this explanation, including the basis for this assessment. The evaluator may provide a synopsis of the defendant's responses to this explanation, may provide direct quotes, or may simply summarize the basis for the opinion that the defendant did or did not understand the notification of rights (e.g., "the defendant was able to paraphrase the explanation"). In addition, the evaluator should document in this section that collateral contacts were also informed of the purpose of the questions asked and the limits of confidentiality.

LEGAL STANDARD
It is useful to cite verbatim the legal standard for CR in the applicable jurisdiction, including the source of that definition (statute or case law). This serves the dual purpose of demonstrating to the

7
chapter

reader that the evaluator is using the proper standard and also helps frame the conclusions offered later in the report.

HISTORICAL INFORMATION

The report should contain *relevant* historical information that was obtained (as described in Chapter 5). In choosing which historical data to include and the level of detail to be provided, the evaluator should be guided by a determination of whether the information is relevant in any way to the elements of CR. For instance, if the defendant is charged with rape, detailed information about his sexual history should be included. However, if the charge is armed robbery, with no sexual overtones, such detail is not likely to be relevant. In addition, the level of detail included about family members should also be guided by relevancy considerations. It may be helpful to note if there is a significant family history of mental illness or criminal involvement (e.g., "the defendant's mother, as well as paternal uncle, and two of his cousins have a documented history of psychiatric treatment for depression"). However, *typically* it is not necessary or appropriate to include names and identifying information about other individuals (e.g., "the defendant's sister, Jane Smith, has multiple arrests for prostitution").

When organizing the historical sections, the evaluator should be guided by the goal of maximizing clarity for the reader. It is usually preferable to organize these sections categorically; for example, family/developmental, education, employment, social (including sexual, marital, relationship), legal, psychiatric, alcohol/substance abuse. The sequencing of these categories should be driven by the particulars of the case. For instance, if a defendant's only psychiatric hospitalizations have occurred during periods of incarceration, it will be clearer to the reader if legal history is provided prior to psychiatric history. It is also clearer, within categories, to present the information in chronologically ascending order.

A summary of the defendant's psychiatric and substance abuse history, including past treatment and response to treatment, is always relevant for a CR report. Similarly, a summary of the defendant's criminal history is likely to be relevant, particularly if the defendant has a pattern of committing crimes similar to the current alleged offense. The extent of detail needed for other areas, such as relationship history, military history, and religious affiliations, will depend on the particular circumstances of the case (e.g., domestic abuse, claims of posttraumatic stress disorder, religious delusions).

MENTAL STATUS/CLINICAL FUNCTIONING

A thorough description of the defendant's clinical functioning and mental status (see Chapter 5) at the time of the evaluation should be provided. If the evaluation is being conducted while the defendant is an inpatient in a psychiatric facility, or is incarcerated, then information about the defendant's course during the period from arrest onward should also be documented, including any psychiatric medications prescribed and response to treatment. Evaluators should provide specific data, rather than just conclusory language, to support the mental status assessment. For example, rather than state that the defendant's reality testing was impaired by delusional beliefs, the evaluator should specify the defendant's particular distortions (e.g., "the defendant claimed that the government implanted a listening device in his molar tooth").

Because a CR evaluation is retrospective, it is helpful in the mental status section to provide data about the defendant's insight, or lack of insight, into past symptoms that are currently in remission. Thus, if the defendant was experiencing hallucinations and delusions at the time of the alleged offense but is recompensated at the time of the evaluation, a description of the defendant's attitude toward these previous symptoms should be noted. For example, rather than simply stating, "the defendant reports no current paranoid thinking" it would be useful to add that "she acknowledged that, around the time of the alleged offense, she believed that her mother was really a witch, but now characterizes that belief as 'crazy . . . I was not taking my medication.' " These types of data will be relevant to the conclusion section, in which the evaluator develops a clinical formulation that accounts for changes over time in the defendant's mental status.

RESULTS OF PSYCHOLOGICAL AND/OR MEDICAL TESTS

Results of all tests performed by the evaluator, or by consultants, should be included in the report. The nature of the tests should be explained as well. Thus, if a Minnesota Multiphasic Personality Inventory (MMPI)-2 was administered, a brief explanation should be offered. The evaluator could explain that this is a self-report test of 567 items that assess psychopathology and personality traits, and that it includes both clinical scales and validity scales. The results should be reported in clear language, comprehensible to a lay person. When reporting on tests that have specific scores (such as the Wechsler Adult Intelligence Scale [WAIS]-III), the results should include a confidence interval. For example, an evaluator could explain that a defendant obtained a full scale IQ score of 100, which indicates that the defendant's actual IQ is most likely within a range of 5 points on either side of that score. Furthermore, the meaning of the score should be explained (e.g., the defendant is functioning within the average range of intelligence).

STATE'S VERSION OF THE ALLEGED OFFENSE

A description of the specific allegations should be provided, based on official documents such as police reports and grand jury minutes. It is not usually necessary to quote the entire police report verbatim. Indeed, often that would be distracting and confusing. A useful guideline is that this section should contain *relevant* information that could inform the CR issue. At a minimum, any data that are indicative of the defendant's mental status, describe specific behaviors, are used as part of the inquiry of the defendant, and/or are referenced in the conclusion section should be documented in this section of the report. If the defendant provided a confession to the police, this should be included, with relevant verbatim quotations.

OTHER PERSONS' DESCRIPTIONS OF THE DEFENDANT OR ALLEGED EVENTS

Relevant data from third parties regarding the defendant's behavior and mental state around the time of the offense should be included at this point in the report. It is particularly important to include factual statements and observations by these individuals, rather than just their opinions/conclusions. For instance, rather than state only that the defendant's wife reported that he was "not in his right mind," this should be augmented by specific examples.

DEFENDANT'S VERSION OF THE ALLEGED OFFENSE

This is a critical section of the report, as it likely will contain data directly focused on the defendant's mental state at the time of the alleged crime. It is therefore necessary to be as accurate as possible and make judicious use of quotes to capture the defendant's version. One long, uninterrupted quotation of the defendant's version is not recommended since, unless the interview was taped and transcribed, it is unlikely that such a lengthy quote is completely accurate. It is also likely that the interview involved some questioning and interruption by the examiner.

This section should also document the evaluator's questions and probing of the defendant, including asking the defendant for his response to specific details included in the police report and/or third party statements. If inconsistencies or discrepancies exist between the defendant's statements over the course of the interview, these should be noted as well. The defendant's report of alcohol or substance use around the time of the alleged offense should also be included, even if the defendant reports no use of drugs or alcohol at the time (e.g., "the defendant reported that he had not been drinking for a week prior to the alleged offense"). Any data or statements about the defendant's version that are referenced and used later in the conclusion section must first be documented in this section.

CLINICAL OPINIONS RELEVANT TO THE ISSUE
OF CRIMINAL RESPONSIBILITY

This is the conclusion section, in which the evaluator offers the clinical and forensic formulation of the case, interpreting the data to address the CR question. As noted earlier, *no new data* should be introduced in this section. Rather, this section should reference previously documented data sources and explain the implications for the conclusions offered.

7
chapter

BEST PRACTICE
Include not only the interpretation and rationale for the conclusions in the report, but also address contradictory data and alternative explanations.

Evaluators should not merely state the conclusions, but should explain how the available data led to them. They should resist the temptation to present the conclusions in a one-sided manner. This issue is specifically addressed in the Specialty Guidelines for Forensic Psychologists (Committee on Ethical Guidelines for Forensic Psychologists, 1991, VII.D): "Forensic psychologists do not, by either commission or omission, participate in a misrepresentation of their evidence, nor do they participate in partisan attempts to avoid, deny, or subvert the presentation of evidence contrary to their own position." Thus, this section should include not only an articulation of the bases for the evaluator's opinion, but also an analysis of contradictory data and alternative explanations that were considered.

In terms of this section's organization, it is recommended that the discussion focus sequentially on the elements of the CR standard. Thus, the first issue would be presence/absence of a mental illness or mental retardation at the time of the alleged offense. That should be followed by an analysis of the relevance of the defendant's mental state to the other relevant legal standards—that is, the particular cognitive and/or volitional prongs in the jurisdiction. If the jurisdiction includes both a cognitive and volitional prong, it is usually clearer to address each of the prongs separately. In addition, the issue of intoxication should be addressed, either to indicate no evidence of a contribution of substance use, or an analysis of the relationship between effects of substance use and the defendant's mental status at the time of the alleged offense.

If the evaluator concludes that the defendant was neither mentally ill nor mentally retarded at the time of the alleged offense, some evaluators would recommend concluding the section without analysis of the cognitive or volitional prongs. The rationale for this position is that, if the foundational element (mental illness/retardation) is not established, then there is no further need for a clinician to analyze the defendant's behavior, as the threshold criterion has not been met. The counter-argument is that the trier of fact may not agree with the evaluator's opinion about this element. The contentious arguments regarding mentally retarded defendants (e.g., *Atkins v. Commonwealth of Virginia*, 2006) provide an excellent illustration of this point, although there are also conflicting opinions in cases involving diagnoses of mental illness. The latter include cases in which diagnostic disagreement occurs, as well as instances in which there may be differences of opinion as to whether the defendant's mental status at the time of the alleged offense rose to the level of a mental illness (e.g., in some individuals with a diagnosis of borderline personality disorder). In these cases, if the evaluator were to discontinue the analysis after offering an opinion on the mental illness/mental retardation element, the report may not provide an adequate basis for testimony. Therefore, it is recommended that, particularly in cases in which there is potential for different opinions regarding whether the legal criteria for mental illness/mental retardation have been met, the opinion section of the report contain a discussion of all the elements of the insanity defense.

The conclusions offered should be tied specifically to the relevant legal standard. Thus, if a jurisdiction employs only the cognitive prong, a discussion of the defendant's impairments in ability to control her behavior is not warranted. A more nuanced issue relates to the language regarding the level of impairment. Many jurisdictions, particularly those that follow the American Law Institute (ALI) standard, refer to "lack of *substantial capacity*" rather than complete impairment. Thus, forensic evaluators in those situations should avoid using absolute terms, such as the defendant was or was not *unable* to appreciate wrongfulness or conform conduct. Rather, they should employ language focusing on the extent of impairment (e.g., "the data suggest that the defendant's capacity was/was not substantially impaired"). Although this may seem like a minor distinction, it could have a significant impact on the assessment of the conclusion's validity. For example, an evaluator might conclude that, despite some evidence of psychopathology, the defendant was not so impaired as to be *unable* to appreciate the wrongfulness of his conduct. The defense attorney in this case may then, under *cross-examination*, undermine this conclusion by forcing the expert to acknowledge that the defendant's ability was impaired to some degree and that perhaps the evaluator was employing too stringent a standard, not consistent with the legal definition. By the same token, the evaluator might conclude that the defendant's symptoms led to his being *unable* to conform his conduct to the law. In that case, the prosecuting attorney will likely elicit data demonstrating that the defendant maintained some degree of control, thus questioning the validity and credibility of the evaluator's opinion.

Articulating the Rationale for Forensic Opinions on Criminal Responsibility

A major element of forensic report writing is the articulation of the relationship between the data obtained and the psycholegal issue. The reader should be able to follow the logic of the analysis tying the conclusions reached to the data reported. A useful schema for evaluating whether the basis for forensic conclusions is adequately articulated was developed by Skeem and Golding (1998) for use with competence-to-stand-trial reports. They characterized the relationship between symptoms and impairment reported in competence reports as either *none, implied, asserted,* or *articulated*. This scheme can be applied to CR reports, adapting their terms for this purpose as follows.

NONE

The evaluator concludes that there was impairment in legally relevant abilities at the time of the alleged offense, but does not describe any relationship between psychopathology and the impairment. Example: "The defendant did not know that her behavior would be considered wrong."

IMPLIED

The evaluator provides data regarding psychopathology but does not then link the psychopathology to a functional impairment, relative to the legal standard for insanity. Example: "The defendant was experiencing paranoid delusions that included a belief that her neighbor was plotting against her."

ASSERTED

The evaluator attributes impairment in legally relevant abilities to psychopathology without specifically describing the relationship. Example: "The defendant's ability to appreciate that her behavior was wrong was impaired by her delusional beliefs about her neighbor."

ARTICULATED

The author clearly specifies the relationship between the psychopathology and the specific functional impairment relevant to the legal standard for insanity. Example: "The defendant was paranoid at the time of the alleged offense, believing that her neighbor was part of a conspiracy to kill her. When her neighbor waved at her, she believed that this was a signal that she was going to be shot, and she stabbed him in order to protect herself. She indicated that she knew that it was illegal to stab someone, but believed that in this case her behavior was legally justified because she was acting in self-defense."

The report should clearly specify how the defendant's mental state did (or did not) influence the relevant abilities, articulating clearly the nexus between the data and the conclusions. In the conclusion section, the evaluator should clarify which particular sources of information were relied upon when citing specific data (e.g., "the arresting officer reported that the defendant was mumbling incoherently and could not understand what he was trying to tell him"). If the evaluator's opinion relies heavily on the defendant's account, on collateral information, or on the results of testing, this should be clearly conveyed so that the trier of fact can decide the validity of those sources. Failure to be clear in this regard undermines the evaluator's responsibility to present the data and conclusions in an objective manner that can be assessed by the trier of fact.

7
chapter

Dealing With Multiple Charges

When defendants are charged with multiple offenses, the evaluator should address the issue of CR separately for each alleged offense, particularly if the analysis might be different for the various offenses. For

BEST PRACTICE

Articulate the relationship between data and conclusions. Also, clarify the sources of information that form the basis of the opinion.

example, Mr. Smith was charged with assaulting two homeless men who, he thought (delusionally), were trying to kill him. After the assault, he went to a police station to complain about the men. When the police did not take him seriously, he picked up a rock and broke a window at the police station. He was thus charged with two counts of assault and battery (A&B) and one count of malicious destruction of property (MDOP). Although the clinical formulation relevant to both offenses was that Mr. Smith was experiencing an acute exacerbation of a chronic paranoid schizophrenic disorder, the relationship between his disorder and each alleged offense differed. For the A&B charges, the evaluator posited a direct relationship between the man's paranoid thinking and his belief that his actions were justified in self-defense. However, for the MDOP charge, the relationship was indirect. His paranoid thinking about the homeless men led him to be frustrated that the police responded in what he considered an inappropriate manner, but he reported that he broke the window out of anger, not related to any distorted thinking about the police. (The analysis could be different if Mr. Smith had reported that he thought the police were part of the conspiracy, but that is a different scenario.)

The recommended format for this type of case (i.e., the offenses occur close in time, and are related) is to present one analysis that deals with the issue of mental illness, and then separate discussions to address the specific CR elements for each of the charges. In other instances, in which a defendant is charged with multiple offenses over a period of several days or weeks, it is important to clarify whether the mental status was similar across time, or whether significant changes occurred that would have had a differential impact on the issue of CR for the separate charges. In such cases, separate analyses of the presence or absence of symptoms of mental illness may be needed.

Ultimate Issue Opinions

One of the most controversial questions in forensic mental health assessment is whether the evaluator should offer an opinion, in the report or in expert testimony, on the ultimate issue being decided by the trier of fact. In CR cases, this refers to addressing whether the defendant specifically meets criteria for being found legally insane. A number of commentators have argued that offering such ultimate opinions strays beyond the bounds of psychological/psychiatric expertise and impinges on the legal and moral decision making of the judge or jury (Morse, 1978; Melton et al., 2007; Heilbrun, 2001; Tillbrook, Mumley, & Grisso, 2003). However, there is some lack of clarity as to what exactly is considered an ultimate issue opinion in CR cases. There is agreement that an evaluator who opines that "the defendant was legally insane" has offered an ultimate opinion. However, an evaluator may instead offer the opinion that "the defendant was substantially impaired in his ability to appreciate the wrongfulness of his conduct." Some would consider this the equivalent of offering an ultimate issue opinion (e.g., Morse, 1978), whereas others would consider this to be a penultimate opinion (e.g., Slobogin, 1989).

Tillbrook and colleagues (2003) propose that forensic evaluators can offer an opinion about the nature and degree of the impairment, but should refrain from offering an opinion that this degree of impairment is "enough" to meet criteria for insanity. Consistent with this position, an evaluator might opine that a manic or paranoid disorder seriously interfered with a defendant's ability to appreciate wrongfulness or conform conduct, without offering an opinion on whether this impairment met criteria for insanity. They reason that no external criterion exists, either based in clinical theory or legal standard, by which to determine how much impairment is "substantial." In referencing insanity evaluations, they specifically comment: "because . . . we do not know how much incapacity is meant by the phrase 'lacked substantial capacity,' any conclusion involving an ultimate opinion perforce transcends the data" (p. 85).

The opposing position has best been articulated by Rogers and Ewing (1989, 2003). They argue that mental health experts do not usurp the roles of triers of fact when they apply their clinical expertise to forensic issues, and that triers of fact are not unduly swayed by experts' ultimate opinions. They argue that a prohibition of ultimate issue opinions has unintended consequences, including obfuscating the expert's data, providing opportunities for expert testimony that is too broad and not relevant to the legal issue, making cross-examination more difficult, and providing more opportunity for the attorneys to distort the expert's testimony. In referring to insanity cases, they provide an example of an expert testifying, based on a WAIS, about a defendant's diminished ability on the comprehension subscale. Since the expert would not be allowed to address the issue of the defendant's ability to "appreciate the wrongfulness of his conduct," the implications of these data for the relevant legal issue would be obscured (Rogers & Ewing, 1989).

Rogers and Ewing also note that, when providing ultimate issue testimony, forensic mental health experts can distinguish between clear cases and borderline ones, in which the data are more ambiguous, but that this distinction will be lost if no conclusory opinion can be provided. Furthermore, they critique the practice of using what they call "semantic brinkmanship," which refers to experts using language that parallels the legal standard but does not use the exact terminology (e.g., opining that a defendant's capacity to conform conduct was "significantly" rather than "substantially" impaired). They argue that such distinctions are not meaningful, and the distinction is not likely to be understood by jurors.

LACK OF CONSENSUS OVER OFFERING
ULTIMATE ISSUE OPINIONS

This controversy has not been settled and, as was noted in the survey by Borum and Grisso (1995) discussed in Chapter 3, no consensus was reached among the psychiatrists and psychologists surveyed. In that study, only 20% of the respondents stated that ultimate issue opinions were contraindicated in criminal forensic reports (with 60% of the psychiatrists and 40% of the psychologists endorsing inclusion of such opinions). The Specialty Guidelines for Forensic Psychologists (Committee on Ethical Guidelines for Forensic Psychologists, 1991)

BEST PRACTICE

Be familiar with the professional literature as well as jurisdictional requirements when considering whether to offer an ultimate issue opinion.

neither endorse nor prohibit such opinions, the American Academy of Psychiatry and the Law (AAPL) Ethics Guidelines for the Practice of Forensic Psychiatry (AAPL, 2005) is silent on the issue, and the AAPL Practice Guidelines for the insanity defense (Giorgi-Guarnieri et al., 2002) specifically state that "there is nothing to prevent its inclusion in a report" (p. S30). Furthermore, some jurisdictions require the forensic mental health clinician to address the ultimate issue in CR cases, whereas others prohibit it (e.g., Federal Rules of Evidence, 704). Thus, evaluators working in this field need to be familiar with both the arguments in the literature and the requirements in their own jurisdictions to guide them about how to deal with this issue.

INADEQUATE DATA AND REFRAINING FROM OFFERING AN OPINION

However, even among psychologists and psychiatrists who endorse providing ultimate issue opinions, there is agreement that such opinions must *not* exceed the data provided. Thus, if the data are not adequate to answer the question, the evaluator should refrain from offering an opinion, on the grounds that such an opinion cannot be offered in that particular case. In such cases, the evaluator should explain in the report the basis for the inability to offer an opinion. This type of situation can occur when conflicting factual data cannot be resolved by a clinician, when the defendant is not able to provide a comprehensive account, or when novel or unusual circumstances exist. As an example of this last point, one could consider the issue of "objective" versus "subjective" wrongfulness discussed in Chapter 2. In most jurisdictions, this issue is unresolved legally. Therefore, in a case in which a defendant appeared to understand that the behavior would be considered wrong by societal standards, but maintained a subjective belief that the act was justified, a forensic clinician would not have a basis for offering an opinion as to whether that legally constituted an impairment in appreciation of wrongfulness. Rather, the evaluator would be able to lay out the issues for

BEST PRACTICE

Do not offer an ultimate issue opinion, even when permitted or required in your jurisdiction, when there are insufficient data to support it.

the court, highlighting the distinction, but leaving it up to the judge to decide which standard would be applied.

ULTIMATE ISSUE OPINIONS AND DIMINISHED CAPACITY/EXTREME EMOTIONAL DISTURBANCE

The guidelines for ultimate issue opinions are much clearer in evaluations of diminished capacity. Some jurisdictions, such as the federal system, explicitly bar ultimate issue testimony in this regard. Even in jurisdictions that do permit such testimony, professional standards (see Chapter 2) do not provide a basis for a forensic evaluator to provide an ultimate opinion in most cases. As Clark (1999) has argued, it is extremely rare for a defendant to have a clinical condition that prevents her from having the capacity to form an intent. Rather, it is more likely that the issue to be addressed is whether the defendant indeed did form the intent. As this is an issue of factual determination for a jury or a judge, forensic clinicians should not offer opinions couched in ultimate language (i.e., "the defendant did/did not form the intent to murder"). Rather, the evaluator may provide an opinion as to whether or not the data are or are not consistent with a level of impairment that could have impacted the defendant's ability to form the requisite intent. (See the discussion of this issue in Chapter 2, relevant to the case of *Clark v. Arizona.*)

In the area of CR evaluation, cases of extreme emotional disturbance (EED), provide perhaps the clearest example of the boundary between clinical and legal conclusions. The standard in EED cases is whether the alleged offense was committed under the influence of an extreme emotional disturbance for which there is a "reasonable explanation or excuse." Although the forensic evaluator can provide an opinion on the nature of the defendant's mental or emotional condition, the issue of whether the resulting behavior was *reasonable* is not amenable to psychological analysis, but is a moral and legal decision to be made by the judge or jury.

Multiple Referral Questions

At times, the referral may involve more than one forensic evaluation question. If the request is for an evaluation of insanity and diminished capacity, these evaluations both refer to the defendant's mental state at the time of the alleged offense. Therefore, no ethical or practical problems are encountered by combining both issues into one report. Indeed, most of the report, including data sections and the clinical formulation, will be relevant to both issues. The report would then contain two conclusion sections, one focusing on the implications of the defendant's mental status for the issue of legal insanity and the other focusing on diminished capacity.

When the referral involves both a CR issue (mental state at the time of the offense) and an evaluation of competence to stand trial, several issues emerge. The CR report focuses on the defendant's mental status in the past, whereas a competence report addresses current mental status and future functioning. However, the most significant issue that arises is that the CR report requires a detailed account of the defendant's version of the alleged offense, which likely contains incriminating information. In competence-to-stand-trial reports, by contrast, incriminating statements from the defendant should not be included. Competence is a pretrial question, so including a defendant's version of the offense could provide the prosecution with self-incriminating information. Even if a state's laws do not allow such pretrial revelations to be used at trial, the prosecution might be led to other incriminating evidence by the defendant's statements (called "fruit of the statement"). The Specialty Guidelines for Forensic Psychology (1991) specifically states that

> Because forensic psychologists are often not in a position to know what evidence, documentation, or element of a written report may be or may lend to a "fruit of the statement," they exercise extreme caution in preparing reports or offering testimony prior to the defendant's assertion of a mental state claim or the defendant's introduction of testimony regarding a mental condition. (p. 663)

Therefore, the ideal solution is to prepare two separate reports in such cases. Typically, the history and current mental status data can be "cut and pasted" between reports, with the remainder of the report focusing on data and reasoning specific to the referral

7
chapter

BEST PRACTICE
Consider submitting separate reports for CR and competence to stand trial, particularly when the mental state defense has not been formally raised.

question that the report is intended to address. The court then has the option to share the competence report with all parties, but permits the CR report to be withheld from the prosecutor until such release is warranted (e.g., once the defendant affirms that an insanity defense will be pursued). In jurisdictions that require that the CR report be shared immediately with the prosecutor, the advantage of separate reports is mitigated. Nevertheless, absent a good reason to combine the reports, the preferred approach is to submit separate reports.

Expert Testimony

Many books and articles provide useful guidance for expert mental health testimony (e.g., Bank & Packer, 2007; Brodsky, 1999; Ewing, 2003). This section focuses on several issues of particular relevance to forensic evaluators testifying in CR cases.

Pretrial Preparation

Although forensic clinicians must begin the evaluation process in a neutral manner, once a conclusion has been reached and testimony is required, the clinician should be prepared to present his opinions in a clear and persuasive fashion. In preparation for this task, the evaluator should consult, prior to trial, with the attorney who will be conducting the *direct examination*. During this pretrial consultation, the following areas, at a minimum, should be discussed.

CURRICULUM VITAE
The witness should provide the attorney with a curriculum vitae and be prepared to explain her relevant education, training, and experience relevant to offering expert testimony on matters of criminal responsibility.

OPINIONS AND LIMITS
The attorney should fully understand the witness's opinion and its limits. The evaluator should explain those elements of the conclusions that support the attorney's position, as well as those that do not.

The evaluator should be explicit in terms of ability and willingness to provide an ultimate issue opinion regarding the CR issue. Furthermore, the evaluator should indicate the specific language that he is prepared to use on the witness stand when asked for an opinion. When the particular facts or circumstances of the case lead the evaluator not to have an opinion, or to have a qualified opinion, this should be clarified as well.

DIRECT EXAMINATION STYLE

The evaluator should inquire about the style of direct examination that the attorney will use. Some attorneys use a highly structured, narrowly tailored style of questioning ("Did you find that the defendant was mentally ill when this event occurred?"), while others will use an open-ended style that provides the expert with more leeway ("Tell us what you found"). Knowing the style of questioning will aid the expert in preparing for testimony.

BEST PRACTICE

Meet with the attorney before the trial to prepare for taking the stand. Make sure to discuss the following:

- Your curriculum vitae
- Opinion to be offered and its limits
- Attorney's style for direct examination
- Any relevant legal rulings
- Psychological tests that were used
- Opinion of the opposing expert
- Possible cross-examination questions

LEGAL RULINGS

The evaluator should learn from the attorney any legal rulings that would have an effect on expert testimony in the case. For instance, if some of the data have been ruled inadmissible, the attorney should make the expert witness aware of this, if possible, prior to testimony. This will allow for better preparation and help avoid missteps on the witness stand. In addition, the expert witness should inquire as to whether the witnesses will be sequestered (not allowed to observe other witness' testimony). This decision is typically made by the court on a case-by-case basis.

PSYCHOLOGICAL TESTING

When psychological testing has been administered, the evaluator should explain the tests to the attorney. This includes information about the nature of the tests, their reliability and validity, as well as any other information that could impact on the admissibility of the methodologies employed (such as peer review, evidence of general acceptance within the field). The evaluator should clarify to the attorney how the testing was used, in terms of the contribution to the clinical and forensic formulation. For example, the attorney could be educated that the Rogers Criminal Responsibility Assessment Scales (RCRAS) does not determine insanity in itself. The evaluator may also explain why any "malingering instrument" used can raise suspicions of malingering but cannot by itself "determine" that the defendant was malingering.

OPPOSING EXPERT'S OPINIONS

If there is an opposing expert, the forensic evaluator should review available reports and discuss with the attorney the areas of agreement and disagreement between the expert witnesses. For example, the experts might agree that the defendant had a particular mental illness at the time of the offense, but have very different opinions about whether and how the illness influenced the defendant's behavior. The evaluator should explain the basis for the difference of opinion to the attorney, to help guide both direct examination and cross-examination. Although the expert witness is typically not serving as a consultant to the retaining attorney (i.e., is not aiding in development of legal strategy, jury selection, etc.), working with the attorney to clarify issues and questions to raise about an opposing opinion is appropriately within the bounds of the expert witness role.

CROSS-EXAMINATION QUESTIONS

The attorney and the witness should discuss possible cross-examination questions with which the witness will have to contend. This will include both substantive and stylistic issues. For example, the attorney may be familiar with the style of the opposing attorney and thus help the witness prepare for the experience. Furthermore, both the attorney and the witness should be prepared for areas of the report that could be challenged and the possible rebuttals that could be made.

Voir Dire

The *voir dire* is the first stage of expert testimony and provides a basis for establishing that the witness can be considered an expert who will subsequently be permitted to provide opinion testimony.

The witness should be prepared to present a vitae and to highlight in testimony his relevant education, training, and experience that bears on the performance of CR evaluations. It is advantageous to have a significant amount of expertise conducting CR evaluations, but every witness has a "first time." It is important for psychologists and psychiatrists to understand, and convey, that their expertise stems not only from their relevant forensic experience, but predominantly from their foundational training in their respective disciplines. Thus, even when testifying for the first time in a trial related to an insanity defense, the evaluator can draw on substantial clinical experience in the diagnosis, assessment, and treatment of psychiatric disorders.

Direct Examination

During direct examination, the evaluator has the opportunity to present the opinions reached and the rationale for those opinions. The evaluator should keep in mind that the judge and/or jury represent a "lay" audience that rarely is knowledgeable about mental health issues and may have significant misperceptions about mental illness. Therefore, the evaluator's role is to educate them about the mental health issues, including diagnoses and symptoms, and the relationship between these and the relevant legal standards for CR. The testimony should be presented in clear, comprehensible language. As with report-writing, overreliance on technical jargon, which is alien to the lay audience, is not desirable. Nevertheless, selective use of technical terms, which are explained clearly, is likely to enhance the expert witness' acceptance as possessing specialized expertise that is beyond the ken of the average juror.

Although expert testimony usually supports the party retaining the expert witness, there are likely to be elements of the opinion that are not helpful to that side. The Specialty Guidelines for Forensic Psychologists (1991) specifically cautions against engaging, whether by acts of commission or omission, in "partisan attempts to avoid, deny, or subvert the presentation of evidence contrary to their own position" (VII.D.). The expert witness cannot volunteer information that is not asked by the attorney, but should not deliberately omit contradictory information. By including all the relevant data in

7
chapter

the written report (which will be available to the opposing side as well), the evaluator minimizes the likelihood that the retaining attorney will be motivated to "hide" contradictory data. It is more effective for the retaining attorney to elicit such testimony on direct examination, which provides opportunity for explanation, rather than allow it to be brought out under cross-examination. In addition to requirements of ethical practice, the credibility and effectiveness of expert testimony is enhanced when the expert is not seen as simply an advocate for one side, but as an objective evaluator.

As discussed earlier, there are opposing views regarding the form of opinion that mental health experts should testify to in CR cases. Although clear consensus exists that mental health experts cannot offer opinions on whether a defendant is guilty or possessed the requisite intent, disagreement arises about whether the forensic clinician should testify that the defendant did or did not meet criteria for legal insanity. Regardless of which approach the expert witness espouses, she must be prepared to explain the rationale for the testimony, including the limits of her willingness or ability to address certain questions posed by the attorney. This is particularly important when the expert does not address the ultimate issue posed, so that the trier of fact is not misled into thinking that the data were ambiguous, but rather understands that the issue is not one the expert believes can be answered by any mental health witness.

Cross-Examination

Bank and Packer (2007) identified a number of standard strategies employed by attorneys to discredit experts during cross-examination. The following are representative examples of strategies as they might arise in CR cases.

LACK OF EXPERTISE
The attorney may attempt to demonstrate that the expert does not have the requisite expertise. As mentioned in the section on *voir dire*, forensic mental health professionals should be prepared to

present their expertise related to conducting insanity evaluations, as well as their clinical experience with relevant populations (e.g., individuals with severe mental illness, substance abusers, correctional inmates, individuals with intellectual disabilities). It is this clinical experience that provides the foundation for the forensic expertise.

FAULTY METHODS

The attorney may question the validity of tests administered and/or the adequacy of the data collection. The witness should be prepared to explain the rationale for any test used in the evaluation. This includes its reliability, validity, error rate, whether it has been subjected to peer review, and whether it has gained general acceptance in the field (Heilbrun, 1992; *Frye v. U.S.*, 1923; *Daubert v. Merrell Dow Pharmaceuticals*, 1993). In addition, the witness should be able to explain the rationale for sources of information obtained and also those not obtained (e.g., "Dr., you contacted three of the witnesses to the alleged offense, why didn't you contact more witnesses?"). An opposing attorney can always think up at least one more source of information that was not sought out. More is not always better, and the witness should be prepared to confidently explain why a particular source was not considered relevant or crucial to the evaluation. If new information is provided, the witness should frankly respond as to whether such new data would impact the opinion offered. However, witnesses should be careful not to speculate about hypothetical situations that are not consistent with the facts of the extant case.

7
chapter

ERRORS IN FACT

The attorney may emphasize any errors noted in the report, even if they are minor. If the opposing attorney demonstrates a factual inaccuracy in the report or testimony, the expert witness should be prepared to acknowledge this error, if true. However, the witness should be prepared to respond by clarifying the significance of the error (i.e., whether the corrected information would impact the conclusions reached). If there was an error in scoring on a test, such as the WAIS-III, the expert should be able to explain if this error in any way impacted the assessment of whether the defendant suffered from a "mental defect." If the clinician notices prior to trial that an error was made, it is best to inform the retaining attorney, so that this can be addressed on direct examination.

PRIOR INCONSISTENT STATEMENTS

Attorneys may attempt to attack the witness' credibility by attempting to demonstrate that their current opinions are different from previously expressed positions. With current information technology, it is not difficult for attorneys to obtain previous publications or presentations by professionals, and these can be used in an attempt to impeach testimony. Experts should be prepared to explain how and why their current opinion may differ from previous positions taken. For example, if the expert has previously opined that an individual with borderline personality disorder was not considered to have a mental illness, but in the current case opines that the defendant with this same diagnosis meets criteria for mental illness, this discrepancy needs to reconciled. The expert may explain, for example, that the current defendant was demonstrating a brief psychotic reaction under stress, as opposed to baseline personality traits.

Even more directly, witnesses should be prepared to explain any testimony that differs from what was written in the report. If new data were obtained following the completion of the report (which did not change the evaluator's opinion, but may have impacted on some elements of the report), the witness should be prepared to explain this and why this new information did not change the conclusions reached. For instance, if the evaluator discovered only after the report was written that the defendant had one previous psychiatric hospitalization, he could explain that this hospitalization occurred many years ago and did not affect the assessment of the defendant's mental status at the time of the alleged offense.

WITNESS BIAS

An attorney may attempt to claim that an expert is biased because he more often offers opinions or testifies for one side (prosecution or defense). An evaluator should be prepared to explain the pattern of her experience as an expert witness. An unbalanced pattern could be a function of the base rate in the population. For example, if, in a particular inpatient setting, only 10% of all defendants evaluated are recommended as meeting the criteria for the insanity defense, this would explain why the evaluator more often testifies for the prosecution. Alternatively, an evaluator may be frequently retained by defense attorneys and often prepare reports *not* supportive of an insanity defense. The evaluator, however, will only be called to testify in those cases in which she opines that the defendant meets the standard. Thus, an expert witness in that case should be prepared to explain that she frequently reaches an opinion that is not consistent with the position of the retaining attorney.

BEWARE
During cross-examination, be prepared for confrontation concerning the following:

- Lack of expertise
- Faulty methods
- Errors in fact
- Prior inconsistent statements
- Witness bias

This is not an exhaustive list of strategies that cross-examining attorneys employ. Rather, it represents some frequently used approaches for which expert witnesses can prepare. The best guiding principle, though, is that the effectiveness of the testimony will be determined not only by skillful and careful adherence to principles of expert testimony (e.g., Brodsky, 1999; Bank & Packer, 2007), but by the quality of the clinical and forensic evaluation that forms the basis for the testimony.

7
chapter

Concluding Comments

The determination that an individual with psychiatric or intellectual impairments should be excused from CR is a legal and moral decision determined by judges and juries, based on criteria developed by legislatures or common law. The triers of fact, however, are dependent on reliable and credible testimony from mental health professionals in order to understand the nature of a particular defendant's impairments and how these may be relevant to the legal standards. Poythress (2004), noting that the empirical literature on CR evaluations is quite limited (see Chapter 3 of this book), has challenged the mental health professions to advocate

BEST PRACTICE

When assessing CR, be sure to

- Conduct a comprehensive forensic evaluation.

- Incorporate the elements identified in the literature.

- Employ appropriate methodologies and tests.

- Use scientific logic in interpreting data (i.e., developing and assessing alternative hypotheses).

- Clearly articulate the relationship between the data obtained and conclusions offered, acknowledging the limitations of the data, when appropriate.

for more research on issues related to the validity of CR evaluations. However, given the present state of knowledge, forensic evaluators can most effectively and ethically provide useful input to the legal system on issues of CR by adhering to the principles discussed in this volume.

Insanity Defense Standards in the 50 States and the Federal System

Jurisdiction	Source of Law	Citation	Standard	Comment
Alabama	Statute	Ala. Code § 13A-3-1	M'Naghten variant	Uses "appreciate" rather than "know"
Alaska	Statute	Alaska Stat. §12.47.010	M'Naghten variant	Omits wrongfulness prong and uses the word "appreciate"
Arizona	Statute	Ariz. Rev. Stat. Ann. § 13-502	M'Naghten variant	Omits "nature and quality" prong
Arkansas	Statute	Ark. Code Ann. § 5-2-312	ALI variant	Omits "substantial" as modifier for capacity; uses "criminality" rather than wrongfulness"
California	Statute	Ca. Penal Code § 25	M'Naghten	
Colorado	Statute	Colo. Rev. Stat. § 16-8-101.5	M'Naghten variant	Omits "nature and quality" prong
Connecticut	Statute	Conn. Gen. Stat. Ann. § 53a-13	ALI variant	Uses "control" rather than "conform" conduct
Delaware	Statute	Del. Code Ann. Tit. 11, § 401(a)	Cognitive prong of ALI	Omits volitional prong

(Continued)

Jurisdiction	Source of Law	Citation	Standard	Comment
Florida	Case law	*Davis v. State*, 32 So. 822 (1902)	M'Naghten	
Georgia	Statute	Ga. Code Ann. § § 16-3-2 and 16-3-3-	M'Naghten variant plus volitional variant	Omits "nature and quality" prong; "delusional compulsion . . . which overmastered his will"
Hawaii	Statute	Haw. Rev. Stat. § 704-400	ALI	
Idaho	Statute	Idaho Code § 18-207	No insanity defense	Abolished defense
Illinois	Statute	720 Ill. Comp. Stat. 5/6-2(a)	Cognitive prong of ALI (variant)	Omits volitional prong; uses "criminality" rather than "wrongfulness"
Indiana	Statute	Ind. Code § 35-41-3-6(a)	Cognitive prong of ALI (variant)	Omits volitional prong; uses "unable" rather than "lacked substantial capacity"
Iowa	Statute	Iowa Code § 701.4	M'Naghten	
Kansas	Statute	Kan. Stat. Ann. § 22-3220	No insanity defense	Abolished defense; *mens rea* defense available
Kentucky	Statute	Ky. Rev. Stat. Ann. § 504.020(1)	ALI	
Louisiana	Statute	La. Rev. Stat. Ann. § 14:14	M'Naghten variant	Omits "nature and quality" prong
Maine	Statute	Me. Rev. Stat. Ann. Tit. 17-1, § 39	Cognitive prong of ALI	Omits volitional prong

(Continued)

Jurisdiction	Source of Law	Citation	Standard	Comment
Maryland	Statute	Md. Criminal Procedure Code Ann. §3-109	ALI (variant)	Uses "criminality" rather than "wrongfulness"
Massachusetts	Case Law	*Commonwealth v. McHoul*, 226 N.E.2d, 556 (1967)	ALI	
Michigan	Statute	Mich. Comp. Laws § 768.21a (1)	ALI (variant)	Includes "nature and quality or the wrongfulness of his or her conduct"
Minnesota	Statute	Minn. Stat. § 611.026	M'Naghten variant	"Nature of act," omits "or quality"
Mississippi	Case Law	*Laney v. State*, 41 So. 2d 216 (1982)	M'Naghten variant	Uses "realize and appreciate" rather than "know"
Missouri	Statute	Mo. Ann. Stat. § 552.030	M'Naghten variant	Uses "knowing *and* appreciating"
Montana	Statute	Mont. Code Ann. § 46-14-102	No insanity defense	Abolished defense; *mens rea* defense available
Nebraska	Case Law	*State v. Hurst*, 592 N.W. 2d 303 (1999)	M'Naghten	
Nevada	Case Law	*Finger v. Nevada*, 27 P.3d 66 (2001)	M'Naghten variant	Ties cognitive prong to delusional state and to appreciating illegality of act; Court reinstated insanity defense that had been abolished by legislature
New Hampshire	Case Law	*State v. Jones*, 50 N.H. 369 (1871)	"Product" test	

(Continued)

Jurisdiction	Source of Law	Citation	Standard	Comment
New Jersey	Statute	N.J. Stat. Ann. § 2C:4-1	M'Naghten	
New Mexico	Case Law	*State v. White*, 270 P.2d 727 (1954)	M'Naghten or volitional component	Volitional: "was incapable of preventing himself from committing it"
New York	Statute	N.Y. Penal Law § 40.15	Cognitive prong only: variant of M'Naghten and ALI	"Know *or* appreciate"; "nature and consequences" substituted for "nature and quality"
North Carolina	Case Law	*State v. Bonney*, 405 S.E. 2d 145 (1991)	M'Naghten	
North Dakota	Statute	N.D. Cent. Code § 12.1-04.1-01	Cognitive prong only	Language substantially different from either M'Naghten or ALI and includes *mens rea* element
Ohio	Statute	Ohio Rev. Code Ann. § 2901.01(A)(14)	M'Naghten variant	Omits "nature and quality" prong
Oklahoma	Statute	Okla. Stat. Ann. 21 § 152	M'Naghten variant	Omits "nature and quality" prong
Oregon	Statute	Or. Rev. Sat.§161.295	ALI variant	Uses "criminality" rather than "wrongfulness"
Pennsylvania	Statute	18 Pa. Cons. Stat. Ann. § 315(b)	M'Naghten	
Rhode Island	Case Law	*State v. Johnson*, 399 A.2d 469 (1979)	ALI	Adds terminology that as a result "cannot justly be held responsible"

(*Continued*)

Jurisdiction	Source of Law	Citation	Standard	Comment
South Carolina	Statute	S.C. Code Ann. § 17-24-10	M'Naghten variant	Omits "nature and quality" prong; specifies that wrongfulness means "morally or legally"
South Dakota	Statute	S.D. Codified Laws § 22-1-2(20)	M'Naghten variant	Omits "nature and quality" prong
Tennessee	Statute	Tenn. Code Ann. § 39-11-501	M'Naghten variant	Uses "appreciate" rather than "know"
Texas	Statute	Tex. Penal Code Ann. § 8.01	M'Naghten variant	Omits "nature and quality" prong
Utah	Statute	Utah Code Ann. § 76-2-305	No insanity defense	Abolished insanity defense; allows special mitigating factor to reduce level of homicide if delusional belief, if true, would have resulted in legal justification
Vermont	Statute	Vt. St. Ann. Title 13 § 4801	ALI variant	Uses "adequate capacity" rather than "substantial capacity" and "criminality" rather than "wrongfulness"
Virginia	Case Law	*Bennett v. Commonwealth*, 511 S.E. 2d, 439 (1999)	M'Naghten or volitional prong	Volitional prong: "totally deprived of the mental power to control or restrain his act"
Washington	Statute	Wash. Rev., Code Ann. § 9A.12.010	M'Naghten	
West Virginia	Case Law	*State v. Grimm*, 195 S.E. 2d 637 (1973)	ALI variant	Omits the word "substantial"; standard is "lack the capacity"

(Continued)

Jurisdiction	Source of Law	Citation	Standard	Comment
Wisconsin	Statute	Wisc. Stat. Ann. § 971.15	ALI	
Wyoming	Statute	Wyo. Stat. Ann. § 7-11-305(b)	ALI variant	Omits the word "substantial"; standard is "lacked capacity"
U.S. Federal	Statute	18 U.S.C.A. § 17	Cognitive prong only; variant of M'Naghten and ALI	Uses "appreciation" as in ALI, rather than know; includes "nature and quality" or wrongfulness as in M'Naghten

Checklist for Criminal Responsibility Reports

I. **Identifying information and referral data**
Identifying information includes, at a minimum

_____ Defendant's name

_____ Date of birth

_____ Date of report

_____ Referral source (e.g., court, defense, prosecution)

_____ Court of jurisdiction

_____ Alleged offenses (including dates)

_____ Type of evaluation (i.e., insanity defense, diminished capacity, extreme emotional disturbance)

_____ Date of court order (if court-ordered)

II. **Sources of information and procedures section**

_____ Interviews with defendant (dates and length of interviews)

_____ Identification of psychological tests or forensic instruments used (if applicable)

_____ Information from records (or note about records requested and not received)

_____ Collateral sources of information

III. Notification of limits of confidentiality/privilege

_____ Defendant informed of the evaluator's role

_____ Defendant informed of purpose of evaluation

_____ Defendant informed of limits of confidentiality/privilege

_____ Data indicating assessment of defendant's understanding of these components

IV. Relevant history includes

_____ Family and developmental history

_____ Educational history

_____ History of adaptations such as work, social (relationships), military

_____ Mental health history, including symptoms, treatment, and response to treatment

_____ Substance abuse history

_____ Criminal justice history

_____ Other history if relevant to the case (e.g., medical, religious)

V. Mental status includes

_____ Appearance, behavior, and relatedness

_____ Mood

_____ Affect

_____ Presence/absence of formal thought disorder/quality of communication

_____ Presence/absence of delusions or other disturbances of thought content

_____ Presence/absence of perceptual disturbances (hallucinations)

_____ Presence/absence of significant cognitive symptoms (memory, attention, concentration, orientation, judgment)

_____ Psychological testing (if appropriate)

_____ Insight into mental illness (if relevant)

VI. Criminal Responsibility Data Sections

_____ Correct citation or reference to appropriate legal standard

_____ Police report of alleged offense (and any other official documents available)

_____ Defendant's version of alleged offense and related timeframe, including detailed probing about specific allegations and mental status at time of alleged offense

_____ Collateral information regarding the alleged offense and of defendant's behavior at the time (if available)

_____ Other clinical details regarding circumstances of offense (e.g., additional mental status data, relationship context, substance abuse, ambiguous fact questions, etc.)

VI. Criminal Responsibility Opinion Section

_____ Clear articulation of basis for opinion on presence/absence of mental illness/mental retardation at time of alleged offense, including assessment of validity of presentation

_____ Clear articulation of relationship between the data and the defendant's capacities relevant to the cognitive prong (insanity defense cases)

_____ Clear articulation of relationship between the data and the defendant's capacities relevant to the volitional prong (insanity defense cases, if applicable)

_____ Clear articulation of relationship between the data and issues relevant to the defendant's ability to form the requisite intent (in diminished capacity or _mens rea_ evaluations)

_____ Role of intoxication (if applicable)

References

American Academy of Psychiatry and the Law. (2005). Ethics guidelines for the practice of forensic psychiatry. Retrieved September 16, 2007 from https://www.aapl.org/pdf/ethicsgdlns.pdf.

American Bar Association. (1983). The insanity defense. *Mental Disability Law Reporter, 7*, 136–141.

American Law Institute. (1985). *Model penal code and annotations.* Washington, DC: Author.

American Psychiatric Association. (1983). APA statement on the insanity defense. *American Journal of Psychiatry, 140*, 681–688.

American Psychiatric Association. (2000). *Diagnostic and statistical manual of mental disorders* (4th ed., text rev.). Washington, DC: Author.

American Psychological Association. (1984). Text of position on insanity defense. *APA Monitor, 15*, 11.

American Psychological Association. (2002). Ethical principles of psychologists and code of conduct. *American Psychologist, 57*, 1060–1073.

Appelbaum, P. (1982). The insanity defense: New calls for reform. *Hospital and Community Psychiatry, 33*, 13–14.

Archer, R. P., Buffington-Vollum, J., Stredny, R. V., & Handel, R. W. (2006). A survey of psychological test use patterns among forensic psychologists. *Journal of Personality Assessment, 87*, 85–95.

Axelrod, B., Barth, J., Faust, D., Fisher, J. M., Heilbronner, R., Larrabee, G., et al.. (2000). Presence of third party observers during neuropsychological testing: Official statement of the National Academy of Neuropsychology. *Archives of Clinical Neuropsychology, 15*, 379–380.

Bank, S. C., & Packer, I. K. (2007). Expert witness testimony: Law, ethics, and practice. In A. M. Goldstein (Ed.). *Forensic psychology: Emerging topics and expanding roles.* Hoboken, NJ: John Wiley and Sons.

Boehnert, C. E. (1989). Characteristics of successful and unsuccessful insanity pleas. *Law and Human Behavior, 13*, 31–39.

Borum, R. (2003). Criminal responsibility. In T. Grisso, *Evaluating competencies: Forensic assessments and instruments* (2nd ed.). New York: Kluwer.

Borum, R., & Grisso, T. (1995). Psychological test use in criminal forensic evaluations. *Professional Psychology: Research and Practice, 26*, 465–473.

Borum R., & Grisso, T. (1996). Establishing standards for criminal forensic reports: An empirical analysis. *Bulletin of the American Academy of Psychiatry and the Law, 24*, 297–317.

Brodsky, S. L. (1999). *The expert expert witness: More maxims and guidelines for testifying in court.* Washington, DC: American Psychological Association.

Callahan, L.A., Steadman, H.J., McGreevy, M.A., & Robbins, P.C. (1991). The volume and characteristics of insanity defense pleas: An eight-state study. *Bulletin of the American Academy of Psychiatry & the Law, 19,* 331–338.

Clark, C. R. (1999). Specific intent and diminished capacity. In A. K. Hess, & I. B. Weiner (Eds.). *The handbook of forensic psychology* (2nd edition). Hoboken, NJ: John Wiley, & Sons.

Cleckley, H. (1941). *The mask of sanity.* St. Louis: Mosby.

Cochrane, R. E., Grisso, T., & Frederick, R. I. (2001). The relationship between criminal charges, diagnoses, and psycholegal opinions among federal pretrial defendants. *Behavioral Sciences and the Law, 19,* 565–582.

Committee on Ethical Guidelines for Forensic Psychologists. (1991). Specialty guidelines for forensic psychologists. *Law and Human Behavior, 15,* 655–665.

Committee on Psychological Tests and Assessment. (2007). Statement on third party observers in psychological testing and assessment: A framework for decision making. Retrieved March 28, 2008 from www.apa.org/science/ThirdPartyObservers.pdf.

Constantinou, M., Ashendorf, L., & McCaffrey, R. J. (2005). Effects of a third party observer during neuropsychological assessment: When the observer is a video camera. *Journal of Forensic Neuropsychology, 4,* 39–47.

Ewing, C. P. (2003). Expert testimony: Law and Practice. In A. M. Goldstein (Ed.). *Handbook of Psychology Volume 11: Forensic Psychology* (pp. 55–66). Hoboken, NJ: John Wiley and Sons.

Fein, R., Appelbaum, K., Barnum, R., Baxter, P., Grisso, T., & Leavitt, N. (1991). The designated forensic professional program: A state government–university partnership to improve forensic mental health services. *Journal of Mental Health Administration, 18,* 223–230.

Fingarette, H. (1972). *The meaning of criminal insanity.* Los Angeles: University of California Press

Fukunaga, K. K., Pasewark, R. A., Hawkins, M. & Gudeman, H. (1981). Insanity plea: Interexaminer agreement and concordance of psychiatric opinion and court verdict. *Law and Human Behavior, 5,* 325–328.

Gaines, A. D. (1995). Culture-specific delusions: Sense and nonsense in cultural context. *The Psychiatric Clinics of North America, 2,* 281–301.

Giorgi-Guarnieri, D., Janofsky, J., Keram, E., Lawsky, S., Merideth, P., Mossman, D., et al. (2002). Practice guideline: Forensic psychiatric evaluation of defendants raising the insanity defense. *The Journal of the American Academy of Psychiatry and the Law, 30,* S3–S40.

Goldstein, A. M., Morse, S. J., & Shapiro, D. L. (2003). Evaluation of criminal responsibility. In A. M. Goldstein (Ed.). *Forensic Psychology, Vol. 11 of the Handbook of Psychology.* Hoboken, NJ: John Wiley and Sons.

Goldstein, A. S. (1967). *The insanity defense.* New Haven: Yale University Press.

Goldstein, R. L, & Rotter, M. (1998). The psychiatrist's guide to right and wrong: Judicial standards of wrongfulness since M'Naghten. *Bulletin of the American Academy of Psychiatry and Law, 16,* 359–367.

Greenberg, S. A., & Shuman, D. W. (1997). Irreconcilable conflict between therapeutic and forensic roles. *Professional Psychology: Research and Practice, 28,* 50–57.

Grisso, T. (2003). *Evaluating competencies: Forensic assessments and instruments.* (2nd ed.). New York: Kluwer.

Grisso, T., Cocozza, J. J., Steadman, H. J., Fisher, W. H., & Greer, A. (1994). The organization of pretrial forensic evaluation services. *Law and Human Behavior, 18,* 377–393.

Grove, W. M., Barden, R. C., Garb, H. N., & Lilienfeld, S. O. (2002). Failure of Rorschach-Comprehensive-System-based testimony to be admissible under the Daubert-Joiner-Kumho standard. *Psychology, Public Policy, and Law, 8,* 216–234.

Halleck, S. (1992). Clinical assessment of the voluntariness of behavior. *Bulletin of the American Academy of Psychiatry and the Law, 20,* 221–236.

Heilbrun, K. (1992). The role of psychological testing in forensic assessment. *Law and Human Behavior, 16,* 257–272.

Heilbrun, K. (2001). *Principles of forensic mental health assessment.* New York: Kluwer.

Heilbrun, K., & Collins, S. (1995). Evaluations of trial competency and mental state at the time of offense: Report characteristics. *Professional Psychology; Research and Practice, 26,* 61–67.

Heilburn, K., Grisso, T., & Goldstein, A. (2008). *Foundations of forensic mental health evaluation.* New York: Oxford.

Heilbrun, K., Marczyk, G., DeMatteo, D., & Mack-Allen, J. (2007). A principles-based approach to forensic mental health assessment: Utility and update. In A. M. Goldstein (Ed.). *Forensic Psychology: Emerging topics and expanding roles.* Hoboken, NJ: John Wiley and Sons.

Heilbrun, K., Warren, J., & Picarello, K. (2003). Use of third party information in forensic assessment. In A. M. Goldstein (Ed.). *Forensic Psychology: Emerging topics and expanding roles.* Hoboken, NJ: John Wiley and Sons.

Hicks, J. W. (2004). Ethnicity, race, and forensic psychiatry: Are we colorblind? *Journal of the American Academy of Psychiatry and Law, 32,* 21–33.

Hurley, K. E., & Deal, W. P. (2006). Assessment instruments measuring malingering used with individuals who have mental retardation: Potential problems and issues. *Mental Retardation, 44,* 112–119.

Kahan, D. M., & Nussbaum, M. C. (1996). Two conceptions of emotion in criminal law. *Columbia Law Review, 96,* 269–374.

Kahneman, D., Slovic, P., & Tversky, A. (1982) *Judgment under uncertainty: Heuristics and biases.* Cambridge: Cambridge University Press.

Kirschner, S. M., Litwack, T. R., & Galperin, G. J. (2004). The defense of extreme emotional disturbance: A qualitative analysis of cases in New York County. *Psychology, Public Policy, and Law, 10,* 102–133.

Knoll, J. L., & Resnick, P. J. (2008). Insanity defense evaluations: Towards a model of evidence-based practice. *Brief Treatment and Crisis Intervention, 8,* 92–110.

Kruh, I, & Grisso, T. (2009). *Evaluations of juveniles' competence to stand trial.* New York: Oxford University Press.

Lally, S. J. (2003). What tests are acceptable for use in forensic evaluations: A study of experts. *Professional Psychology; Research and Practice, 34,* 491–498.

Levine, R. E., & Gaw, A. C. (1995). Culture-bound syndromes. *The Psychiatric Clinics of North America, 3,* 523–536.

Lilienfeld, S. O., Wood, J. M., & Garb, H. N. (2000). The scientific status of projective techniques. *Psychological Science in the Public Interest, 1,* 27–66.

Melton, G. B., Petrila, J., Poythress, N. G., & Slobogin, C. (2007). *Psychological evaluations for the courts: A handbook for mental health professionals and lawyers.* 3rd ed. New York: Guilford Press.

Morey, L.C., Warner, M.B., & Hopwood, C.J. (2007). The Personality Assessment Inventory: Issues in legal and forensic settings. In A. M. Goldstein (Ed.). *Forensic Psychology: Emerging topics and expanding roles.* Hoboken, NJ: John Wiley and Sons.

Moran, R. (1981). *Knowing right from wrong: The insanity defense of Daniel McNaughten.* New York: The Free Press.

Morse, S. J. (1978). Crazy behavior, morals, and science: An analysis of mental health law. *Southern California Law Review, 51,* 527–564.

Morse, S. J. (1979). Diminished capacity: A moral and legal conundrum. *International Journal of Law and Psychiatry, 2,* 271–298.

Morse, S. J. (1984). Undiminished confusion in diminished capacity. *Journal of Criminal Law and Criminology, 75,* 1–55.

Morse, S. J. (1994). Causation, compulsion, and involuntariness. *Bulletin of the American Academy of Psychiatry and Law, 22,* 159–180.

Nicholson, R. A., & Norwood, S. (2000). The quality of forensic psychological assessments, reports, and testimony: Acknowledging the gap between promise and practice. *Law and Human Behavior, 24,* 9–44.

Nickerson, R. S. (1998). Confirmation bias: A ubiquitous phenomenon in many guises. *Review of General Psychology, 2,* 175–220.

Nisbett, R. E., & Wilson, T. D. (1977) Telling more than we can know: Verbal reports on mental processes. *Psychological Review, 84,* 231–259.

Ogloff, J. R. (1990). The admissibility of expert testimony regarding malingering and deception. *Behavioral Sciences and the Law, 8,* 27–43.

Otto, R.K., Banres, G., & Jacobson, K. (1996). The content and quality of criminal forensic evaluations in Florida. *Presented at American Psychology-Law Society Conference, Hilton Head, S.C.*

Otto, R. K., Slobogin, C., & Greenberg, S. A. (2007). Legal and ethical issues in accessing and utilizing third-party information. In A. M. Goldstein (Ed.). *Forensic Psychology: Emerging topics and expanding roles.* Hoboken, NJ: John Wiley and Sons.

Packer, I. K. (1983). Post-traumatic stress disorder and the insanity defense: A critical analysis. *Journal of Psychiatry, & Law, 11,* 125–136.

Packer, I. K. (1987). Homicide and the insanity defense: A comparison of sane and insane murderers. *Behavioral Sciences and the Law, 5,* 25–35.

Packer, I. K. (2008). Specialized practice in forensic psychology: Opportunities and obstacles. *Professional Psychology: Research and Practice, 39,* 245–249.

Packer, I. K., & Leavitt, N. (1998). Designing and implementing a quality assurance process for forensic evaluations. *Presented at American Psychology-Law Society Conference,* Redondo Beach, CA.

Pasewark, R. A., & Pantle, M. (1979). Insanity plea: Legislators's view. *American Journal of Psychiatry, 136,* 222.

Petrella, R. C., Benedek, E. P., Bank, S. C., & Packer, I. K. (1985). Examining the application of the guilty but mentally ill verdict in Michigan. *Hospital and Community Psychiatry, 36,* 254–259.

Petrella, R. C., & Poythress, N. G. (1983). The quality of forensic evaluations: An interdisciplinary study. *Journal of Consulting and Clinical Psychology, 51,* 76–85.

Phillips, M. R., Wolf, A. S., & Coons, D. J. (1988). Psychiatry and the criminal justice system: Testing the myths. *American Journal of Psychiatry, 145,* 605–610.

Poythress, N. G. (2004). Reasonable medical certainty: Can we meet Daubert standards in insanity cases? *Journal of the American Academy of Psychiatry and the Law, 32,* 228–230.

Quen, J. Q. (1994). *The psychiatrist in the courtroom: Selected papers of Bernard L. Diamond, M.D.* Hillsdale, NJ: The Analytic Press.

Raifman, L. (1979). Interjudge reliability of psychiatrists' evaluations of criminal defendants' competency to stand trial and legal insanity. *Presented at the American Psychology-Law Society Conference,* Baltimore.

Rogers, R. (1984). *Rogers Criminal Responsibility Assessment Scales (RCRAS) and test manual.* Odessa, FL: Psychological Assessment Resources.

Rogers, R. (1987). The APA position on the insanity defense: Empiricism vs. emotionalism. *American Psychologist, 42,* 840–848.

Rogers, R., & Ewing C. P. (1989). Proscribing ultimate opinions: A quick and cosmetic fix. *Law and Human Behavior, 13,* 357–374.

Rogers, R., & Ewing C. P. (2003). The prohibition of ultimate opinions: A misguided enterprise. *Journal of Forensic Psychology Practice, 3,* 65–75.

Rogers, R., Gillis, J. R., & Bagby, R. M. (1990). The SIRS as a measure of malingering. A validation study with a correctional sample. *Behavioral Sciences and the Law, 8,* 85–92.

Rogers, R., Gillis, J. R., Dickens, S. E. & Bagby, R. M. (1991). Standardized assessment of malingering: Validation of the Structured Interview of

Reported Symptoms. *Psychological Assessment: A Journal of Consulting and Clinical Psychology. 3*, 89–96.

Rogers, R., & Shuman, D. W. (2000). *Conducting insanity evaluations* (2nd ed.). New York: Guilford Press.

Skeem, J., & Golding, S.(1998). Community examiners' evaluations of competence to stand trial: Common problems and suggestions for improvement. *Professional Psychology: Research and Practice, 29*, 357–367.

Slobogin, C. (1989). The "ultimate issue" issue. *Behavioral Sciences and the Law, 7*, 259–266.

Smith, G. A., & Hall, J. A. (1982). Evaluating Michigan's guilty but mentally ill verdict: An empirical study. *Journal of Law Reform, 16*, 75–112.

Sparr, L. F., & Atkinson, R. M. (1986). Posttraumatic stress disorder as an insanity defense: Medicolegal quicksand. *American Journal of Psychiatry, 143*, 608–613.

Steadman, H. J., McGreevy, M. A., Morrissey, J. P., Callahan, L. A., Clark Robbins, P., & Cirincione, C. (1993). *Before and after Hinckley: Evaluating insanity defense reform.* New York: Guilford Press.

Stock, H., & Poythress, N. G. (1979). Psychologists' opinions on competency and sanity: How reliable?. *Paper presented at American Psychological Association Annual Convention.*

Strasburger L. H., Gutheil T. G., & Brodsky A. (1997). On wearing two hats: Role conflict. *American Journal of Psychiatry, 154*, 448–456.

Teichner, G., & Wagner, M. T. (2004). The Test of Memory Malingering (TOMM): Normative data from cognitively intact, cognitively impaired, and elderly patients with dementia. *Archives of Clinical Neuropsychology, 19*, 455–464.

Tillbrook, C., Mumley, D., & Grisso, T. (2003). Avoiding expert opinions on the ultimate legal question: The case for integrity. *Journal of Forensic Psychology Practice, 3*, 77–87.

VandenBos, G. (2006). *APA Dictionary of Psychology.* Washington DC: American Psychological Association.

Vitacco, M. J., & Packer, I. K. (2004). Mania and insanity: An analysis of legal standards and recommendations for clinical practice. *Journal of Forensic Psychology Practice, 4*, 83–95.

Warren, J. I., Murrie, D. C., Chauhan, P., & Morris, J. (2004). Opinion formation in evaluating sanity at the time of the offense: An examination of 5175 pre-trial evaluations. *Behavioral Sciences and the Law, 22*, 171–186.

Weiner, I.B. (2007). Rorschach assessment in forensic cases. In A. M. Goldstein (Ed.). *Forensic Psychology: Emerging topics and expanding roles.* Hoboken, NJ: John Wiley and Sons.

Wettstein, R. M. (2005). Quality and quality improvement in forensic mental health evaluations. *Journal of the American Academy of Psychiatry and the Law, 33*, 158–175.

Wiederanders, M. R., Bromley, D. L., & Choate, P. A. (1997). Forensic conditional release programs and outcomes in three states. *International Journal of Law and Psychiatry, 20,* 249–257.

Zapf, P. A., & Roesch, R. (2009). *Evaluation of Competence to Stand Trial.* New York: Oxford University Press.

Ziskin, J., & Faust, D. (1995). *Coping with psychiatric and psychological testimony* (5th ed.). Los Angeles: Law and Psychology Press.

Zusman, J., & Simon, J. (1983). Differences in repeated psychiatric examinations of litigants to a lawsuit. *American Journal of Psychiatry, 140,* 1300–1304.

Tests and Specialized Tools

Halstead-Reitan Neuropsychological Battery (Reitan, 1979)
Luria Nebraska Neuropsychological Battery (Luria, 1965)
M-FAST: Miller Forensic Assessment of Symptoms Test (Miller, 2001)
MCMI-III: Millon Clinical Multiaxial Inventory-III (Millon, 1994)
MMPI-2: Minnesota Multiphasic Personality Inventory (Butcher et al., 2001)
PAI: Personality Assessment Instrument (Morey, 1991)
RCRAS: Rogers Criminal Responsibility Assessment Scales (Rogers, 1984)
SIMS: Structured Interview of Malingered Symptomatology (Smith & Burger, 1997)
SIRS: Structured Interview of Reported Symptoms (Rogers, Bagby, & Dickens, 1992)
Stanford-Binet Revised, Fourth Edition (Thorndike, Hagen, & Sattler, 1986)
TAT: Thematic Apperception Test (Murray, 1943)
TOMM: Test of Memory Malingering (Tombaugh, 1996)
VIP: Validity Indicator Profile (Frederick, 1997)
WAIS-III: Wechsler Adult Intelligence Scale, Third Edition (Wechsler, 1997)
WASI: Wechsler Abbreviated Scale of Intelligence (Psychological Corporation, 1999)

References for Tests and Specialized Tools

Butcher, J. N., Graham, J. R., Ben-Porath, Y. S., Tellegen, A., Dahlstrom, W. G., & Kaemmer, B. (2001). *Minnesota Multiphasic Personality Inventory–2 (MMPI-2): Manual for administration and scoring* (Rev. ed.). Minneapolis: University of Minnesota Press.

Frederick, R. (1997). *The Validity Indicator Profile*. Minneapolis, MN: National Computer Systems.

Luria, A. R. (1965). Neuropsychological analysis of focal brain lesion. In B. B. Wolman (Ed.), *Handbook of clinical psychology*. New York: McGraw-Hill.

Miller, H. A. (2001). *Miller-Forensic Assessment of Symptoms Test (M-FAST): Professional manual*. Odessa, FL: Psychological Assessment Resources.

Millon, T. (1994). *Manual for the Millon Clinical Multiaxial Inventory (MCMI–III)*. Minneapolis, MN: National Computer Systems.

Morey, L. C. (1991). *Personality Assessment Inventory: Professional manual*. Odessa, FL: Psychological Assessment Resources.

Murray, H. A. (1943). *Thematic Apperception Test manual*. Cambridge, MA: Harvard University Press.

Psychological Corporation (1999). *Wechsler Abbreviated Scale of Intelligence*. San Antonio, TX: Author.

Reitan, R. M. (1979). *Manual for administration of neuropsychological test batteries for adults and children*. Tucson, AZ: Author.

Rogers, R. (1984). *Rogers Criminal Responsibility Assessment Scales (RCRAS) and test manual.* Odessa, FL: Psychological Assessment Resources.

Rogers, R., Bagby, R. M., & Dickens, S. E. (1992). *Structured Interview of Reported Symptoms (SIRS) and professional manual.* Odessa, FL: Psychological Assessment Resources.

Smith, G. P., & Burger, G. K. (1997). Detection of malingering: Validation of the Structured Inventory of Malingered Symptomatology (SIMS). *Journal of the American Academy of Psychiatry and the Law, 25,* 183–189.

Thorndike, R. L., Hagen, E. P., & Sattler, J. M. (1986). *The Stanford–Binet Intelligence Scale: 4th edition. Technical manual.* Chicago: Riverside Publishing.

Tombaugh, T. N. (1996). *TOMM: The Test of Memory Malingering.* North Tonawanda, NY: Multi-Health Systems.

Wechsler, D. (1997). *Wechsler Adult Intelligence Scale* (3rd ed.). San Antonio, TX: Psychological Corporation.

Cases and Statutes

Ake v. Oklahoma, 470 U.S. 68 (1985).

Atkins v. Commonwealth of Virginia, 272 Va. 144 (2006).

Bieber v. People, 856 P. 2d 811 (1993).

Clark v. Arizona, 126 S. Ct. 2709 (2006).

Commonwealth v. Stroyny, 435 Mass. 635 (2002).

Commonwealth v. Baldwin, 686 N.E.2d 1001 (1997).

Daubert v. Merrell Dow Pharmaceuticals, Inc., 509 U.S. 579 (1993).

Durham v. U.S., 214 F.2d 862 (1954).

Edney v. Smith, 425 F. Supp. 1038 (1976).

Federal Rules of Evidence (2007).

Frendak v. U.S., 408 A.2d 364 (1979).

Frye v. U.S., 293 F. 1013(1923)

Houston v. State, 602 P.2d 784 (1979).

Insanity Defense Reform Act of 1984, 18 U.S.C. §17.

Jones v. U.S., 463 U.S. 354 (1983).

Kane v. U.S., 399 F.2d 730 (1968).

Kumho Tire v. Carmichael, 526 U.S. 137 (1999).

Lee v. County Court of Erie County, 267 N.E.2d 452 (1971).

McDonald v. United States, 312 F.2d 347 (1962).

M'Naghten case, 8 English Reporter 718 (1843).

Montana v. Egelhoff, 518 U.S. 37 (1996).

New York v. Schmidt, 110 N.E. 945 (1915).

Parker v. State, 254 A.2d 381 (1969).

People v. Conley, 411 P.2d 911 (1966)

People v. Conrad, 385 N.W.2d 277 (1986).

People v. Goldstein, 843 N.E.2d 727 (2005).

People v. Kelly, 516 P.2d 875 (1973).

People v. Larsen, 361 N.E.2d 713 (1977).

People v. Lim Dum Dong, 78 P.2d 1026 (1938).

People v. Poddar, 518 P.2d 342 (1974)

People v. Rittger, 355 P.2d 645 (1960).

People v. Stress, 252 Cal. Rptr. 913 (1988).

People v. Toner, 187 N.W. 386 (1922)

Porreca v. State, 433 A2d 1204 (1981).

Rex v. Arnold, 16 How. St. Tr. 695 (1724).

State v. Crenshaw, 659 P.2d 488 (1983).

State v. Hamann, 285 N.W.2d 180 (1979).

State v. Hartfield, 388 S.E.2d 802 (1990).

U.S. v. Alvarez, 519 F.2d 1036 (1975).

U.S. v. Brawner, 471 F.2d 969 (1972).

U.S. v. Cameron, 907 F.2d 1051 (1990).

U.S. v. Segna, 555 F.2d 226 (1977).

U.S. v. Frisbee, 623 F. supp. 1217 (1985).

U.S. v. Pohlot, 827 F.2d 889 (1987).

Wade v. U.S., 426 F.2d 64 (1970).

Key Terms

actus reus: Latin term, meaning "bad act," referring to the act that is an element of a criminal offense.

American Law Institute (ALI) standard: a standard for an insanity defense, proposed in the Model Penal Code, that states that a defendant will be found Not Guilty by Reason of Insanity, if "as a result of mental illness or mental defect he lacked substantial capacity either to appreciate the wrongfulness of his conduct or to conform his conduct to the requirements of the law" (ALI, 1985).

competence to stand trial (CST): a legal doctrine that requires meaningful participation of criminal defendants in their defense at various stages of the proceedings by requiring that defendants possess specific relevant capacities.

conditional release: a system, used in a number of states, to allow insanity acquittees to be discharged from a hospital under specified conditions that, if violated, can result in revocation of their release to the community.

criminal responsibility (CR): related to the mental state of the defendant at the time of an offense; encompasses both complete defenses to a crime (such as the insanity defense) as well as partial defenses such as diminished capacity and extreme emotional disturbance.

cross-examination: questioning by the attorney who did not call the witness, typically adversarial.

deific decree: refers to an individual acting in response to what he or she believes is a command from God.

diminished capacity defense: a defense to a crime based on an assertion that the defendant lacked the capacity to form the specific intent required as an element of the crime.

direct examination: questioning by the attorney who called the witness, typically supportive.

extreme emotional disturbance (EED): a defense, used in only a minority of states, that can result in reduction from a charge of murder to a finding of manslaughter if the act was "committed under the influence of extreme mental or emotional disturbance for which there is reasonable explanation or excuse" (ALI, 1985, Section 210.3[1][b]).

forensic assessment instrument (FAI): structured quantitative interview tool designed for focused assessment of the functional legal abilities of direct relevance to legal questions.

Guilty but Mentally Ill (GBMI): a verdict that involves a finding that the defendant committed the crimes but did so while mentally ill; this still results in a conviction.

Incompetent to Stand Trial (IST): a legal finding in which a given defendant is identified as lacking in the abilities necessary to meaningfully participate in a relevant stage(s) of the proceedings.

mens rea: Latin term meaning "guilty mind," referring to the mental elements required for conviction of a crime, in addition to the *actus reus*.

M'Naghten standard: the standard for insanity developed in England, which states that a defendant will be found Not Guilty by Reason of Insanity if, due to mental disease or defect, he did not "know the nature and quality of the act he was doing or if he did know it, that he did not know he was doing what was wrong" (M'Naghten case, 1843).

Not Guilty by Reason of Insanity (NGRI): a legal determination that an individual will not be held responsible for an act based upon the individual's mental state at the time of the commission of the act; the specific criteria for such a determination are defined by applicable statutes or case law.

product standard: an insanity defense standard in which a defendant will be found Not Guilty by Reason of Insanity if the behavior was a product of a mental illness or mental defect.

psychopath: a person with a specific form of personality disorder, not included in the *DSM-IV-TR*, involving a callous, egocentric personality style, coupled with an impulsive, chronically antisocial lifestyle.

response style: the subtle or overt motivational approach used by an examinee during an evaluation that can significantly impact the data obtained; for example, some examinees may respond with full honesty and full effort, some may distort the results in an effort to appear a certain way, and others may put forth minimal effort in their responses.

sociopath: *See psychopath.*

ultimate issue opinion: an opinion offered by an expert witness directly addressing the legal determination to be made by the court.

voir dire: a term used to refer to a preliminary examination of a witness by the attorneys, to determine whether the witness will be allowed to provide expert testimony on a specific topic.

volitional impairment: an individual's substantial inability to control his or her behavior.

Index

About the Author

Ira K. Packer, PhD, is currently clinical professor of psychiatry at the University of Massachusetts Medical School (UMMS), and serves as director of the UMMS Forensic Psychology Postdoctoral Fellowship Program. He is the author or co-author of a number of articles including issues related to the insanity defense, expert witness testimony, and training and practice in forensic psychology. He also has presented seminars and workshops on developing quality assurance measures for criminal forensic reports at national conferences and at the invitation of a number of state mental health departments. In his capacity as Chair of the Forensic Specialty Council, he was the lead author of the Education and Training Guidelines for Forensic Psychology.

Dr. Packer has been engaged in the practice of forensic psychology for almost 30 years, and served as Assistant Commissioner for Forensic Services, Massachusetts Department of Mental Health. He is board certified in forensic psychology by the American Board of Professional Psychology. He has previously served as president of both the American Board of Forensic Psychology and the American Academy of Forensic Psychology. He received the 2007 Distinguished Contributions to Forensic Psychology award from the American Academy of Forensic Psychology.